SEX, TEMPTATION, AND MODESTY

I0459141

SEX, TEMPTATION, AND MODESTY

A BIBLICAL VIEW OF INTIMACY

RICK THOMAS

SEX, TEMPTATION, AND MODESTY:
A Biblical View of Intimacy

ISBN 978-1-966741-06-0

Rick Thomas

© 2025 Life Over Coffee

Unless otherwise noted, all Scripture references herein are from the English Standard Version, copyright © 2001 by Crossway, Inc. Used by permission. All rights reserved.

No part of this publication may be reproduced, stored in a retrieval system, or transmitted in any form or by any means without the express written permission of Life Over Coffee.

Edited by Sarah Hayhurst

Life Over Coffee
8595 Pelham Rd Ste 400 #406,
Greenville, SC 29615
LifeOverCoffee.com

Romans 12:1-2
I appeal to you therefore, brothers, by the mercies of God, to present your bodies as a living sacrifice, holy and acceptable to God, which is your spiritual worship. Do not be conformed to this world, but be transformed by the renewal of your mind, that by testing you may discern what is the will of God, what is good and acceptable and perfect.

For additional resources, visit
lifeovercoffee.com

Table of Contents

Introduction

Romans 12:1-2 is part of the Apostle Paul's letter to the Christians in Rome. In these verses, he is transitioning from the doctrinal discussions in the earlier chapters to practical applications of those teachings in the lives of believers. It would be wise for today's Christians to study and heed the apostle's teaching, and I hope this small treatment on sex and temptation will assist from an application perspective. Paul begins by appealing to the believers based on the mercies of God, which he has elaborated on in the preceding chapters (1-11). These mercies include God's gracious act of providing salvation through faith in Jesus Christ, forgiveness of sins, and the promise of eternal life. This appeal suggests that the response to God's mercy should be one of action and dedication on the part of the believer.

In the Old Testament, sacrifices were central to worship, involving the offering of animals or other goods to God. Paul uses this imagery to call for a different kind of sacrifice: believers offering their own lives to God. Unlike the dead sacrifices of animals, Christians are to offer themselves as living sacrifices. This lifestyle means living in a way that is holy (set apart for God) and pleasing to Him, which Paul describes as the true or rational (logical) form of worship. It signifies a total dedication of one's life to God's service.

Paul warns the believers in his day against adopting

the values and behaviors of the worldly society that are opposed to God's ways, which involves resisting societal pressures to behave in ways that contradict God's teachings. Instead of conforming to worldly patterns, believers are to be transformed, which begins in the mind—the source of all our sin patterns. It involves a complete change in how one thinks, leading to behavioral change. This mind renewal enables believers to understand and discern God's will—what is good, pleasing, and perfect. The ultimate goal of not conforming and being transformed is so that believers can understand God's will. We must recognize what is morally good, pleasing to God, and in line with His perfect plan and purposes. Romans 12:1-2 calls for a radical reorientation of the believer's life in response to God's mercy—a wholehearted commitment to God, marked by a life that is distinct from the world's ways and aligned with God's will, achieved through ongoing transformation that starts from within.

In this book, I aim to avoid the pitfalls of legalism where the Christian mimics the behaviors of cold-hearted religion while not succumbing to cultural pressures to be like the world. We want to address our hearts while seeking God to learn what is acceptable and pleasing to Him. Our marching orders come from His mind and will, not the traditions of the culture or religion.

Rick Thomas

1

Too Much Skin, Girl

While summer is an appreciated and welcomed relief from the blistering cold of winter—for those of us who have winters—it does bring a different difficulty to our lives. The summer months draw attention to our universal struggle with sex, sexuality, and temptation, with the modesty debates taking a prominent role in our conversations. The knee-jerk reaction is to blame our fallen counterparts without careful consideration of what the Bible says regarding universal depravity and every human's temptation to turn what God intended for good into something that will tantalize our lust-filled desires. The sober-mindedness of the mature believer considers personal responsibility and communal input. These careful Christians understand sin's complexities and their common blindspots that do not discriminate.

A Common Problem

We live in a highly sexualized culture that acts as though it cannot get enough of the provocative. Pornography is without question the all-time sexual leader when it comes to capturing the hearts and minds of our global culture. Porn is the most lucrative and largest industry on the

Internet, and it's the most-oft-used marketing approach when selling products to our culture. Sex sells. Christians and non-Christians are head-over-heels in love with the human body. Sex has gripped the hearts of our teenagers and has infected the minds of too many parents. Whether it's the stay-at-home mom who serial posts her latest hair style to her following or the triple-X pornographer, we love ourselves and cannot wait until we can show the world the best side of ourselves.

Rarely is there a week that goes by where I'm not dealing with a person, couple, or family whose sexually related problems have ripped them apart. No one is free from its temptations or its effects, which is why I hope that as you read, you do not fall into the trap of finger-pointing—especially toward the other gender. We are collective failures regarding sex and sexuality. Our humility as we approach our common curse will affect how we process and proceed through this book. Maybe the words of Jesus will be helpful as you think about this emotional and sometimes touchy subject of modesty.

> Why do you see the speck that is in your brother's eye, but to not notice the log that is in your own eye? Or how can you say to your brother, 'Let me take the speck out of your eye,' when there is the log in your own eye? You hypocrite, first take the log out of your own eye, and then you will see clearly to take the speck out of your brother's eye.
> (Matthew 7:3-5)

Some men will indeed lust at any female, at any time, and for any reason, just because she is breathing and walking upright. As some women lamented: "I could put a burlap sack over my body, and a man would still lust after me." I agree with the despairing statement—at least for how it applies to some men—but it would be myopic to think that every man is this way or that what a woman wears does not matter. The problem with sexual temptation is far more complicated than male gender issues, and if our first impulse is similar to Adam's: "That woman you gave me" (Genesis 3:12), then you've lost the plot. Sensuality is a multi-layered problem because porn comprises internal (the heart) and external (the body) dynamics. The issue's complexity should be a call for every Christian to dialogue as friends rather than gender competitors.

Our Mutual Fall

If a man chooses to lust after a woman, it is his fault, not hers. It is his choice, and Jesus had strong language for such a person: he should pluck out his eyes (Matthew 5:29-30). We know Jesus was using hyperbolic language, but that does not remove the seriousness of the problem. Ever since the fall of Adam, there have been two functional realities in our lives: God gave men the desire to notice the opposite sex, and being attracted to the beauty of a woman should be a good thing. Satan's deception has turned the man into a selfish individual; he now has a hostile adversary, which is lust. God's good creation of love is flipped upside down as it tempts men to twist love into lust. Women have their problems, too. When Satan slithered into the Garden of Eden, he did not leave the woman unscathed.

Like Adam, she took the Lord's kind gifts and turned them into her version of perversion. God made her attractive. Her beauty draws the attention of a man, and every woman knows it. You can tell by how Christian women present themselves on their favorite social media platforms. The Lord did not create her to disgust a man each time he looks at her. She wants him to look at her, to like her, and to love her. Satan's deception twisted these good things into bad things. Her desire for someone to love her tempts her to use her appearance to capture the gaze of a man to fill heart longings that only the Lord can satisfy. The inherent Adamic weaknesses in men and women tempt them to take God's good gifts of beauty and sexual attraction and twist them into self-serving agendas.

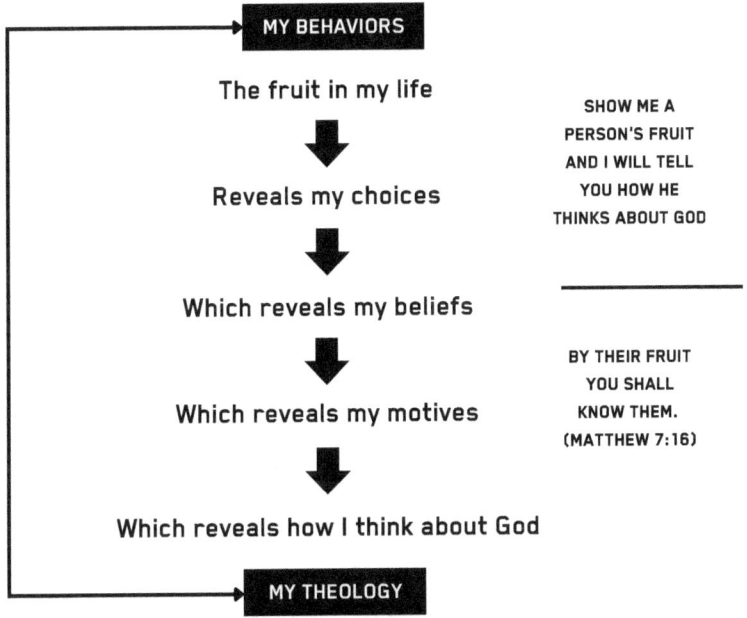

MY BEHAVIORS

The fruit in my life

SHOW ME A PERSON'S FRUIT AND I WILL TELL YOU HOW HE THINKS ABOUT GOD

Reveals my choices

Which reveals my beliefs

BY THEIR FRUIT YOU SHALL KNOW THEM. (MATTHEW 7:16)

Which reveals my motives

Which reveals how I think about God

MY THEOLOGY

This universal temptation means modesty matters. How you present the beauty of Christ externally to others is just as important as how you carry the beauty of Christ in your heart. Your external life reveals what is growing in your heart (Luke 6:45; Matthew 7:16). There is no discontinuity or disconnectedness between how you paint your face and present your latest hairstyle, what you wear, and what is happening in your heart. Notice the infographic and how it illustrates how the fruit in our lives reveals our thoughts, motives, and, ultimately, how we think about God. You can properly deduce from this illustration that what is happening in a person's heart will manifest as comparable fruit in their lives: if lust is in the heart, there will be an object of lust in their sight line.

I'm a Signpost

He must increase, but I must decrease.

(John 3:30)

A few years ago, Lucia and I were in a small group where a woman, a wife and mother, wore mini-shorts with the all-caps word PINK written across her bottom. It was impossible for anyone not to look at least once, and it mattered not if it were a male or female, child or adult. She was a provocative signpost, telling everyone in the room to look at her backside. Her message could not have been clearer: "Hey Y'all, Look at my bum!" She reminded me of men who wear hyperbolic belt buckles that draw attention to their crotches. Sadly, this lady was new to our group, and nobody knew her well enough to pull her aside to talk to her about her neon ad-wear. It was an awkward moment for all of us, and in hindsight, perhaps we should have offended her, but we chose not to.

> *Do not let your adorning be external—the braiding of hair, the wearing of gold, or the putting on of clothing—but let your adorning be the hidden person of the heart with the imperishable beauty of a gentle and quiet spirit, which in God's sight is very precious.*
>
> (1 Peter 3:3-4)

She accomplished her agenda: every eye in the place, including the women and children, got a screenshot of her rear end, something you could not unsee. Rather than drawing attention to the Lord, she was drawing attention to herself. She is one of a zillion examples of women who dress in such a way not only to devalue themselves but also to take away from the imperishable beauty that the apostle Peter extolled. She chose to praise herself, unlike John the Baptist, who considered himself a signpost in the wilderness with one mission in life: to point others to Christ. When you see a sign, you read it, process it, and do what it is telling you to do. You do not give the sign a second thought; it's not about the sign but the message. We have one job: point people to Jesus.

I am not the Christ, but I have been sent before him.
(John 3:28)

The signpost knows its job. Unfortunately, this lady was a self-absorbed signpost whose primary interest was to redirect the minds of the men in the room from the Christ she professed to her bottom that she was proud of. If a woman dresses in such a way as to draw attention to herself, she is tempting those around her to sin. If the man does sin, it is his fault, but the woman bears culpability. She needs to know how she is a temptress—assuming she does not already know. We cannot say this is just one gender's problem. We must be talking about this social contagion while humbly dialoguing about God-centered solutions. It is not suitable for a man to place all the blame on a woman. It is just as wrong for a woman to make this exclusively a man's problem.

Objectification of Women

A woman's culpability regarding our universal problem with sex and sexuality is one of the things that is so perplexing about insecure, pre-meditative women and the Internet. For example, Danica Patrick, the former female NASCAR driver, believed she could compete with the men and demanded that men respect her. Okay, fair enough.

You're welcome to compete with the men if you wish. That's an argument for another day. However, it's disingenuous to expect us to respect her while she provocatively devalued herself by performing striptease GoDaddy commercials in the early part of the 2000s. Ripping off part of her clothing makes no sense if the message is R.E.S.P.E.C.T.

Of all the people in the world who could do a GoDaddy ad, it had to be a woman who takes her clothes off while women scream at us not to objectify them. It's a contradiction of purpose. Women rightfully lament how they do not want men objectifying them while insisting that we respect them for what they can do. I completely agree with both points, but Danica presented the perfect illustration of the "you can't have it both ways" dilemma. Danica was a famous example of what many of the women in our church gatherings do each Sunday. I don't want to objectify any woman, but it would be helpful if some of these women cooperated with this good aim. What Danica did was the equivalent of teaching a weight loss class at McDonald's. It is wrongheaded to decry a man's sexual perversions when you're guilty of trying to be sexually appealing.

While women can be provocative in their clothing choices, men can be calculatingly secretive about their temptations, too. Most men stuck in porn do not give their wives or their friends full access to their world. Wife, if your husband indeed has nothing to hide, there is no reason for you not to have complete access to all of his devices. He should be willing to talk to you about his temptations with lust. I am not suggesting your husband is a porn addict, but I am saying he was born in Adam, which means he came into this world totally depraved. Even if he has been "born a second time," he is not free from sin's temptations (Ephesians 4:22). You do not have to be addicted to pornography to be affected by sexual sin. The wise and humble couple will seek to have an open dialogue about their temptations because they recognize that these two things are not a news flash:

- Husbands have been affected by the fall, which means our understanding and practice of sexuality is not entirely pure.
- Husbands do struggle to some degree with sexually related issues. None of us are entirely pure regarding sex and sexuality.

A mature husband will want to talk to his wife about his temptations. A mature woman will want to be part of her husband's sanctification—especially in the area of the most intimate part of their lives.

My Brother's Keeper

Discretion will watch over you, understanding will guard you.

(Proverbs 2:11)

Dear Christian,

I urge you to reflect on how you dress. Whether male or female, it is our Christian duty to point others to Christ, not to ourselves. The desire of our hearts should be to give people something to think about rather than how we look or what we wear. Sometimes, it is better to exercise self-control by setting aside our personal preferences for the glory of God. Discretion is a godly trait that will watch over us while protecting us from evil. Husbands and wives should pursue honesty and transparency within their marriages. Perhaps your marriage is not in a place where it can handle these kinds of truths. Possibly due to the shaping influences of your past, you're not at a point where you can talk at this level of Christian maturity. If that is true for you, find your starting point, wherever it may be, and start talking to each other. Husband, your wife deserves to know about you, and she should have the opportunity to care for your soul, just as you should be willing to care for her.

Call to Action

1. Though you may not be interested in capturing the gaze of a man, do you understand how your beauty can be a snare to a man?
2. Are you willing to make whatever necessary and prudent changes to serve the men in your sphere of influence?
3. Does your wife have full access to all your devices? If not, why not?
4. Does your wife have appropriate access to your thoughts about your battles with lust? If not, why not?

2

Backward Porn Addiction

Most of us understand the traditional definition of porn addiction. Typically, it's in the context of a guy lusting after a girl. Active lust toward another person is the primary way porn is acted out in our culture, but it is no longer the exclusive twisted domain of men who won't control their eyes and actions. There is another kind of porn addiction that is unique to women. It's a backward porn addiction, as one lady told me during a counseling session. This porn addiction carries a similar idea of lusting, but directionally it's different—the woman wants men to look at her. She attempts to capture the eyes of a man.

Backward Porn Addiction

A backward porn addiction is when a person intentionally attempts to lure the gaze of another person through physical manipulation, either by what they are wearing or by how they look. The hidden motive of the heart is that if she can draw attention to herself, she will feel better about herself. I never heard the term—though I am familiar with the concept—until I was discipling a couple with marriage problems a few years ago. The wife began to talk about her struggles with what she called a backward porn addiction.

I was amazed more by her humility than by the term. She shamefully shared how she found a perverse pleasure in capturing the gaze of guys. It gave her a secret power surge that filled a void in her soul. She talked about her fixation on her appearance. This over-concern about her physicality had leeched into other sinful areas of her heart. The result was that she dressed for other people rather than for the Lord.

She also talked about how she felt affirmed and appreciated when guys looked at her. Though she knew what she was doing was sinful, and her presupposition regarding love had become twisted (2 Corinthians 10:3-6), she did not know how to change, or stated differently, the satisfaction of the craving was stronger than her desire to change (James 1:14-15). She struggled with life-long battles of insecurity, which was a carryover from her former manner of life that she brought into her new life with Christ (Ephesians 4:22). Instead of doing the hard work of changing, she chose a much easier path of dressing in such a way that tempted others to notice—especially men. Her surprising humility opened the door for a few questions, which she was eager to discuss. For this chapter, I will reformat some of my questions to her to give you an opportunity to reflect on your motives about modesty, clothes, appearance, fellow image-bearers, and God.

- When you dress in the morning, do you think more about God's gaze upon you or other people's gaze?
- Do you dress to put the Lord's name on display or your physicality on display?
- How does the glory of God impact your thought life when it comes to your appearance?
- Would your closest friends (or spouse) say you are overly concerned about how you look?
- Can you leave your residence without being sinfully controlled by how you look?

- Are you free to not wear make-up?
- Do you secretly compare yourself to other women?
- What feeds your thinking more: how the culture views beauty or how God thinks about beauty?

Checking Out the Competition

My friend was not actively pursuing traditional porn avenues, though she was hooked on a feeling that motivated her to feed her porn addiction in a backward kind of way. Her reverse porn addiction led to other ancillary sins that connected to her core heart problem. Sin never plays fair, and once it crosses the threshold of our hearts, it will seek to devour its prey by destroying every room in our hearts. One of those ancillary sin problems was the subtle pleasure of feeling smug (self-righteous) in her judgments about dirty men who looked at porn. How ironic. Because her addiction was not as overt as dirty old men looking at porn, her reasoning ran along these lines: "Guys are sleazy. They disgust me with the way they gawk at women."

While her assessment was correct about lust-hungry, dirty old men who fill their lust cups through gawking, her choice to dress in such a way as to draw attention to herself was not more spiritual, biblical, or honoring to God. Her self-righteous posturing and hair-splitting had dulled her conscience to the point of self-deception (Hebrews 4:7-8). Two people's porn addictions may be going in different directions—forward and backward—but both of them have corrupted and captured souls that snatch God's glory for self-glorification. Mercifully, my friend was self-aware and self-disclosing. She talked about how a backward porn addiction manifests itself differently. She mentioned three specific ways:

- People who compare themselves to others (2 Corinthians 10:12).

- People who compete against others (Philippians 2:3-4).
- People who crave the approving gaze of others (Proverbs 29:25).

She told me how it's a common practice when women are in a small group to check out the other people in the group. While some women do this for ideas about clothing or maybe because they enjoy the way their friend dresses, there is a darker side to people gazing, and she was humble enough to say the quiet part aloud. She said, "We are checking out the competition to see how we compare. We want to see what the other woman has or if what we have is better." The apparent heart issue that she was identifying was insecurity, a fear that motivates someone to be overly concerned about how they look. My friend was referring to the other woman's physique.

> Not that we dare to classify or compare ourselves with some of those who are commending themselves. But when they measure themselves by one another and compare themselves with one another, they are without understanding.
>
> (2 Corinthians 10:12)

The Sad Runners-Up

Paul suggested that a person like this is without understanding; it's a nicer way of saying they are fools. The line of thinking suggests that if she were more attractive, she would feel better about herself. Of course, it's a stronghold waiting to happen: if she does not look as good as other women, the temptations of envy, jealousy, anger, bitterness, or even depression will soon follow. These insecure women who cannot compete with those they believe are prettier will find the fatal flaw in the other women, which gives their self-righteous souls a boost. At least they can look down on those they deem prettier. They never see the pitfall: there will always be a prettier woman. The beauty gods have blessed these "superior women," or they have tricked the beauty gods through human engineering to where nobody can compete with them.

Unable to meet the beauty standards of the elite leads to despair for the runners-up. Always comparing yourself to others is one of the reasons porn is so devastating to a woman. In her mind, she cannot compete with what her husband is looking at on the Internet. And she can't! It's like competing with the Marvel universe. There is Plasti-woman, Insta-girl, and ready-for-action cyber babe—the fake people our delusional culture grades as perfect tens. No sane woman can compete with that kind of instant fake-ness, and no biblical-minded woman would want to, which is why adultery is so excruciating. Adultery shatters a wife's world because she knows—among many other things—that the competition has ousted her.

I appreciated my friend's honest and transparent willingness to make the conversation about her need for change rather than hijacking the counseling session as a ruse to hide her hidden heart idolatries. She could have because our meetings were due to her husband's porn addiction. After several weeks of counseling and much-needed work in her husband's heart, the kind Counselor (Spirit of God) turned the light on her. She did not have to say what she told me. Imagine if she had not. No doubt, her husband would have found help, which he did, and changed. But they would have gone home with a dirty little secret—in her heart. God would not let her alone, and she would no longer resist what He was doing in her.

Capturing a Man's Gaze

Most people have a hard time discussing a worldview that is so thought-exposing. She was revealing the secret handshake among the fraternity of women, but what she shared was not the entire story. There is another plot twist to her porn addiction. A backward porn addiction is more than checking out the competition to feel superior to them or drown in despair because of them. Another aspect of this addiction is a woman's subtle desire to capture the gaze of a man. Gaze capturing can be a deceptive and appealing drug for an insecure woman. She feels a sense of power when she makes a man look more than once. Though she may be disgusted at the thought of adultery, she is flattered by his gaze.

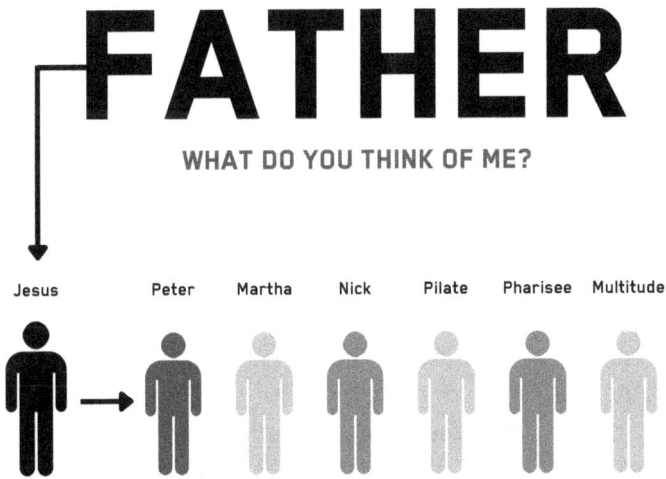

FATHER

WHAT DO YOU THINK OF ME?

| Jesus | Peter | Martha | Nick | Pilate | Pharisee | Multitude |

I'm no longer afraid of you; I can biblically love you.

Her soul was in a battle over opinions: What do other men think of me, or what does God think of me? Whose opinion will manage her? Whose opinion will drive her clothing choices? Whose eyes or attention will she attempt to attract? These questions are triggering and tempting. They say there is nothing wrong with trying to feel sexy or look attractive. These women drone on by laying the entire problem in the man's lust if he looks too long. Yes, it is the man's fault if he lingers too long, but it is naive and deceptive to refuse any responsibility for fellow image-bearers. Everyone knows when they are manipulating someone, which is a gift of God's Spirit to bring such gentle reminders about our motives and actions. No Christian should be that detached from their real motives, including our sinful ones.

> Therefore, if food makes my brother stumble, I will never eat meat, lest I make my brother stumble.
>
> (1 Corinthians 8:13)

Let me paraphrase Paul in 1 Corinthians 8:13: "Therefore if the way I dress makes my brother stumble, I will never dress in a way that may capture his attention, lest I make my brother stumble." The impulsive person responds, "I could dress in a burlap sack, and a man would lust after me." Probably. Some men. However, when the argument immediately shifts toward others without careful consideration of yourself, you've already crossed biblical lines (Matthew 7:3-5). Lustful men lust. True. The more humble starter question should model my friend who had every right to lambaste her porn-searching husband, but her heart was not so hard to where she could not hear the Spirit's voice (Hebrews 3:7). Do you dress in a way that seeks to capture the gaze of a man? Will you honestly and humbly answer the question? If you are genuinely unsure, will you ask someone their perspective about how you present yourself to the public? Would you ask the Lord to give you the grace and courage to assess the way you take care of your body? These questions would make an excellent conversation between husbands and wives, as well as a good discussion for a small group of women.

Looking for Shepherds

This problem does not land squarely on women, though this chapter is about my humble friend identifying a universal struggle with so many of our sisters. However, a woman's body appearance and clothing selections are also a leadership responsibility for the men in their lives, especially husbands and dads. Perhaps a few insightful questions for husbands and dads would provide a leadership opportunity for them, too.

- Dad, how are you shepherding your daughters regarding their temptations toward sensuality?
- Husband, are you aware who is "hitting on your wife"?
- Is your wife "eye candy" for others?
- How are you guarding your wife's heart and reputation?
- Are you guilty—in part—of how she appears before others?
- Do you know the difference between being culturally relevant and sensually tempting?
- Are you engaging and envisioning the females in your home about these things?

I'm sure you know that the ladies in your home struggle with insecurity. The biblical record affirms that all people—male and female—struggle with some form of fear of man (Proverbs 29:25). Our culture is relentless in presenting what is perfect when it comes to our bodies. Their targeted marketing and our sense of Adamic shame form a crippling mindset that can take the strongest heart captive. Having this awareness should motivate us to index into proactivity because we already know the ladies in our homes do care about what others think about them. Thus, we must be intentionally redemptive in their lives, engaging them about their temptations, motivations, and the grace of God.

Mable's Beauty Trap

Mable's parents said she would never go to the mailbox without putting on make-up. They saw this as a positive character trait. They were glad that she cared about herself. Her parents were undiscerning. Fear of man controlled Mable: what people thought about her mattered more to her than anything else, even God's favorable opinion of her. She was a fearful idolator who believed she needed to pay close attention and exacting detail to how she looked to others. Rather than shepherding her through this life-dominating sin pattern, Mable's parents applauded her desire to be attractive. Her insecurity and emptiness grew. Trying to maintain a high level of beauty for people's approval is for the insecure person, like what crack is for the addict. Mable needed to be freed from the beauty trap and reacquainted with the gospel.

> For by grace you have been saved through faith. And this is not your own doing; it is the gift of God, not a result of works, so that no one may boast.
>
> (Ephesians 2:8-9)

Not only are Christians saved by grace, but grace is the means through which sanctification happens. The Christian's complete salvation—including sanctification—is a gift from God. The insecure person, who is in bondage to the beauty trap, will seek to overcome their problem through self-effort by over-caring about what they look like or what they wear. Suppose Mable did overcome her insecurity by making herself beautiful enough to feel better about herself. She would still be in bondage because she would only be as strong as her ability to stay beautiful. She could even fake humility by talking about how she overcame her insecurity, as her eyes go to the floor while shuffling her feet and giving glory to God. "Oh, He's been so kind to me." But she would always have a low-grade awareness of losing her ability to stay beautiful forever (2 Corinthians 1:8-9, 4:7, 12:7-10).

Beauty's deception and accompanying legalism create a formidable tandem. It's an insatiable fixation that leads to more sinful and painful manipulations. The primary deception is that she will react to her insecurity by competing with her culture, hoping to manipulate her friends while appeasing the beauty gods. She'll misdiagnose the real battlefield: she's in a tug-o-war with the only one who can free her (James 4:6). God wants to release her from the grips of a controlling culture so she can find peace in Him alone. Freedom comes through weakness, not strength or beauty (2 Corinthians 12:10).

Call to Action

1. Husband, is your wife susceptible to a backward porn addiction? How do you know?
2. Dad, is your daughter becoming addicted similarly? If so, will you come alongside them to care for them? Ask the Father to give you the insight and opportunity to speak with them. Learn, love, and lead them to a more effectual and practicalized outworking of the gospel. There is a truer, purer, and more powerful beauty found in Christ (1 Peter 2:3-4).
3. Ladies, I provided several questions throughout this chapter. Will you go through them and take them to the Lord, asking Him to expose to you what He already knows about you (Hebrews 4:13)? Will you find a friend to help you unhook from the bondage of people's control—if this is a sinful temptation for you?

3

Men and Women Temptations

Though it would be simpler to place the lust problem in the lap of one gender, it would bring harm to God's Word because lust is every person's temptation. Perhaps a couple of synonyms for lust will level the playing field, holstering our tongues to where we're less likely to go, "Ready! Fire! Aim!" and react more soberly as we consider the wisdom in the sequence of the log and speck (Matthew 7:3-5). I was thinking about these things when I received this letter from a friend.

> *Dear Rick,*
>
> *I have gone through the trauma of discovering that my husband was viewing pornography. I thought it was a problem that only involved explicit material. I never knew or even thought that any unproperly dressed woman was tempting him to sin. Then he began confessing to me that he was lusting after any woman on the street, our church, and even our family magazines—those who exposed themselves with inappropriate clothing. I was shocked and horrified. The pain and suffering we went through were the worst things that ever happened in my life. BTW, God healed me of cancer. The saddest thing*

of all was that I never knew how men looked at women or what they thought when they looked. Knowing this broke my heart. I never knew how the clothing of a woman affected the men around me.

My husband never told me how it affected him. I followed the secular way of clothing myself without realizing how I was contributing to the problem. Bikinis, shorts, cleavage, and tight-fitting jeans that accentuate lower body parts all were some of the things that tempt men to lust and sometimes to yield to that temptation. Can you see how deceived I was? Worst of all, I thought I never looked like them—those who were unashamedly trafficked in porn. I was under the impression that my clothing was tasteful and sophisticated. I was completely oblivious to how what I had on affected the men and women around me. Call me naive, but I never knew that our fathers, husbands, brothers, and pastors lusted after women. I thought it was only the unsaved and perverted people who "really" needed Jesus. But it was in my church, my home, and my marriage.

My appeal is to our leaders, husbands, and fathers to help us, protect us, and lead us. Tell us what it is about our unacceptable clothing. Tell us why it is unacceptable. Tell us what it is all about. Tell us how we can cause men to stumble. Tell us what is happening in the minds of the men around us. If you will speak honestly to us and love us enough to tell us the truth about porn, many wives and daughters will be grateful and willing to humble themselves into more God-centered ways of thinking and dressing. Many husbands are not leading their wives this way. Many mothers are not modeling modesty to their daughters. I fear for the next generation of wives, mothers, and daughters who will be even more naked than they are now.

The enemy deceives us into thinking that pornography in the media is the problem. We women, mostly through our ignorance, have become part of the problem, and nobody seems to be willing or prepared to speak openly about it. I thank God Almighty for the power of the blood of Jesus that took my husband out of bondage and restored our marriage. Now, I dress very attractively for my husband in private. The moment we leave our home, I change into a modern, trendy lady, but not a sexy one. This process works very well for us. When you dress sexy in public, you will be dressing sexy for the public. I don't want to be an object of lust. Do not be deceived: God is not mocked, for whatever one sows, he will also reap.

[Mable]

Let's Go Deeper

For the one who sows to his own flesh will from the flesh reap corruption, but the one who sows to the Spirit will from the Spirit reap eternal life.

(Galatians 6:8)

READER WARNING: If you interpret this chapter as an attempt to blame a man's lust problems on women, you've misinterpreted the purpose of the chapter, and I appeal to you to ask God to provide the clarity you need to discern the point, as Mable painfully articulated. Each person is entirely responsible for the sin they commit. Nobody is allowed to blame their sin on others, on circumstances, or as a by-product of living in a fallen world. Porn is a two-way street. It takes two people to engage in porn. The guy who is seeking a sexual object to satisfy his lust and a woman who wants to be the object of his lust. Remove either participant, and porn would struggle to survive.

Typically, when people think about porn, they quickly jump to the perverted guy problem, which is only half of the equation, which is why Mable—the wife of a porn addict—

wrote to me. She made a vigorous and compelling appeal for me to talk about the other side of the porn problem—the gaze capturers. Before I proceed, may I ask you a question: When I say "porn" or "pornography," what comes to your mind? I asked my wife this question, and she said, "Naked women." She did not jump to the perverted guy problem but talked about women with no clothes on. What she conveyed is the other misunderstanding about the porn problem: that it's only about the naked women found on the Internet, adult movies, and porn magazines.

Thinking that porn is only a perverted guy problem or a naked lady problem not only narrows the interpretation of porn to something that misses a vital detail, but it reduces the Bible's impact on the real issue. To understand the real problem, you have to go deeper than the outward manifestation of the problem—the dude looking or the woman unclothed. Looking below the surface is how we address all our problems; we begin in the heart before we address the behavior, which is why the Bible starts at the root of porn rather than its fruit. Jesus said it this way:

> I say to you that everyone who looks at a woman with lustful intent has already committed adultery with her in his heart.
>
> (Matthew 5:28)

Reframing the Problem

You cannot get into porn without first lusting for it, which begins in the heart. Porn participation is the overflow of lust-filled hearts. Thus, understanding the underlying heart issue not only broadens the scope of porn, but it's an alarming warning to women everywhere that millions of husbands, fathers, brothers, and leaders are tempted to lust even if they never look at porn. James gets to the heart of the matter when he says,

Each person is tempted when he is lured and enticed by his own desire (lust). Then desire when it has conceived gives birth to sin (porn), and sin when it is fully grown brings forth death [relational dysfunction].

(James 1:14-15)

A lady in a church building on Sunday morning is better than her being on the set of an X-rated production, but her church building is not impervious to the encroachments of lust. Her role in our ubiquitous battle against the entanglements of lust is just as essential in the sanctuary as it is at her swimming pool. Any woman is a potential lust magnet that can attract a guy because this kind of sensual temptation does not isolate itself on the Internet. Unlike the alcoholic, who can take another route to work rather than drive by the liquor store each morning, lust is harder to escape. After you re-frame the conversation from the behavioral problem that it most certainly is to a deeper heart issue, you will be able to perceive how much bigger it is while being able to fortify yourself in the fight.

Without dismissing or minimizing the man's temptation to lust or removing all the responsibility he deserves when he acts out on that temptation, it is just as important to give adequate time to the other side of this problem: women enjoy being observed, and they hope someone will find them attractive. God put an attraction gene in both the male and female. In Genesis 1 and 2, the concept of looking at a girl and being liked by a guy was God's design. Adam was the pursuer, and Eve was what he wanted. And it was good. Then the man and the woman fell hard in the garden. Sin opened Adam's eyes in ways he could never have imagined before, and Eve walked in her unique-to-her darkness. They both enjoyed their versions of perversion.

Providing Conduits to Porn

Adam wanted Eve for self-serving purposes. Eve desired Adam to pursue her for self-serving purposes. Eve's sin is why women are easily tempted to seduce or manipulate a man. For some women, it is because they enjoy the tantalizing power they can exert over a guy. I'm sure this is not an odd thought to you, especially if you contextualize that desire within the feminist movement. Feminists like Eve hate the role of submission, which is why they rebelled like their predecessor. Do you believe this temptation to manipulate or gain power is exclusive to the feminist lobby? There are millions of women who love God, but sin tempts them to manipulate the opinions of others by how they present themselves to others. These women are gaze capturers.

Are you a gaze capturer? Do you secretly enjoy the power (perverse security) you feel when people notice you? Do you secretly enjoy the ability to control (perverse security) others by your beauty? Just as darkness filled Eve's godly desire to be pursued and enjoyed by Adam at the dawn of sin, a post-modern godly woman can also be tempted by the pleasure that lust offers and the power it promises. More than likely, you have not posed in a pornographic magazine or starred in a pornographic movie. However, do you believe you are less guilty than the woman who does if you dress in a way that tempts a man to sin after you? Certainly, you may be less guilty from a consequential perspective. Still, if you dress in a way that tempts a man to sin, you are minimally acting as a conduit that feeds his lust until he can find more explicit satisfaction somewhere else.

Like the wife who wrote me, you can unwittingly cooperate with the porn person by the way you dress. My appeal would be for you to guard your heart against thinking the porn queen is the only problem in the battle against lust. It is possible for a church-going, God-loving woman to play a role in lust's victories. While I'm not your judge, I would appeal to you to talk to your husband, your father, your pastor's wife, your small group leader's wife, or some other godly person who is willing to speak into your life lovingly. If you are not dressing in a way that is alluring, tempting, manipulating, seducing, or gaze-capturing, you have nothing to worry about and nothing to change. However, if you are, wouldn't it be great to know now? Wouldn't humility motivate a Christ-centered response from you? I realize this brings up a whole other set of problems in the Christian community, so let me ask about those who care for you.

Who is Your Faithful Friend?

Faithful are the wounds of a friend; profuse are the kisses of an enemy.

(Proverbs 27:6)

One of the sadder observations I have seen in the Christian community is the lack of loving courage that is required to bring the corrective care that this kind of problem demands. The proverbial faithful friend is more of an anomaly than a ubiquitous reality. Sadly, when there is corrective care, it happens with harshness and carelessness rather than restorative love that leaves the person built up in the faith. Individuals freed by the gospel act like the gospel. In the context of this discussion, there are two essential characteristics of this kind of gospel care and freedom. The caregiver brings corrective care in a spirit of gentle love that is courageous, compassionate, complete, and constructive. The care-receiver wants their corrective care because the gospel has delivered them from the desire to hide, fear, or self-protect.

If either one of those conditions does not happen, friends will not be faithful to each other, which brings us to two important questions: Are you freed by the power of the gospel to be a faithful friend? Are you freed by the power of the gospel to ask a faithful friend to evaluate your clothing choices? If you are free to ask a friend for help, you may press the point further by sharing some of your darker temptations with that person. Make it easy for them to care for you. Rather than expecting them to ask you the perfect question, you can circumvent this potential pitfall in caregiving by being proactive through self-disclosure while releasing them from having to land the perfect question.

Hey, Good Looking

Most of us women are not even sure what is inappropriate anymore. We have given over to following the media, the fashion gurus, and Hollywood.

– [Mable]

One of the more significant tensions in the modesty wars is our misunderstanding of what it means to look desirable. Usually, the point of focus gets hung up on the word desirable, as in, "Are you saying I should not look desirable?" Most certainly, it is a good thing to look desirable and to want someone to desire you. That is living according to how God designed you; He made Eve desirable, and Adam desired her. To be undesirable could be a hindrance to the gospel's effectiveness: we would run from each other. The real issue here is not about being desirable but about whose authority you are going to submit to as the definers of what is desirable. It is a sad commentary on the church that our culture is doing the trend-setting within the church. The only people in the world with the right answers about modesty should be setting the pace and establishing the trends, at least within our Christian culture.

Call to Action

1. When you think about the porn problem, what is the first thing that comes to your mind, i.e., perverted men, naked women, or something else?

2. Have you considered the source of porn, which is lust from the heart? Why is it vital to reflect on this problem at its source?

3. Do you realize how you cannot confine lust to the porn industry? Please explain why you answered as you did.

4. Because lust is omnipresent, what is your responsibility in fighting against its encroachments?

5. Because lust is omnipresent, what specific way do you lust? (Think about your cravings, sinful desires, or things that have more control over your thoughts than Sovereign Lord.) This question may be the most important one for you to answer. Our most powerful sin pattern is self-righteousness, which manifests by finding someone we can condemn. It's easy to compare our sins with others. Paul said, "There is none righteous, no not one."

4

Why Men Struggle

Sex is a beautiful thing. A sinful sexual temptation is not, but giving in to sexual temptation is worse. As fallen creatures, though redeemed by God, these temptations will always be part of our human experience. After the fall of Adam and Eve in the Garden of Eden, every person has struggled with distorted views of sex and sexual temptation. These problems are some of the universal assumptions you can make about anyone. We assume such things because of fallenness but not out of condemnation. We have a mutual understanding of our human condition and need for transformative grace. In this chapter, I will be addressing every man's battle with sex.

Not Free, Indeed

When someone asked a humble, godly, old Christian what it is like to be free from sexual temptation, his response was, "I don't know. I will let you know when that time comes." You don't want to dismiss the old, godly man's perspective on sexual temptation as an anomaly. I was there when he said it. He had an impeccable reputation and was a saintly stalwart in the Christian community for decades. He is with Jesus now, but at the end of his life, he still battled with sexual temptation. How do you think about those who are not free from sexual temptation? Of course, I'm making a distinction between ubiquitous temptation and succumbing to it. Living with temptation means you're very much alive.

When some people think about sexually tempted people, they immediately relegate them to the perverted regions of human depravity. That kind of thinking is unsophisticated, unkind, and unhelpful. To cast every sexually tempted person under the bus of perversion is immature, ignorant, and arrogant (self-righteous). Sexual temptation is a universal temptation for men (and women) because it is supposed to be. The Lord built into the man a desire to like and enjoy the opposite sex. It would have been a major relational faux pas if the Lord created man without a desire for a woman. Placing naked Eve in front of naked Adam and for Adam to not like what he was looking at would have been weird. I suppose Adam could have thanked the Lord for giving him a helper and went out to play with the animals.

> And the rib that the LORD God had taken from the man he made into a woman and brought her to the man. Then the man said, "This at last is bone of my bones and flesh of my flesh; she shall be called Woman, because she was taken out of Man." Therefore, a man shall leave his father and his mother and hold fast to his wife, and they shall become one flesh. And the man and his wife were both naked and were not ashamed.
> (Genesis 2:22-25)

Enjoying Eve

But Adam did not go out and play with the animals. He wanted to play with his new playmate. You hear it in his voice: "At last." I have someone I can connect with, a person with whom I can relate. Eve was different from the rest of God's creative work. She was different from Adam, which made them perfect for each other. They fit like a hand in a glove. You sense this in the instinctive attraction he had for her. She was different, and he desired her. Sometimes, when people talk about sexual temptation, they don't go back far enough. If they do go back at all, they only go back to Genesis 3, where man's view and practice of sex was distorted and depraved by sin.

If you're going to talk about sex, the essential place to begin is how sex and sexual relationships were always supposed to be. Sex was good, and Adam and Eve enjoyed their sexual relationship. They were not ashamed. Naked and sharing the most intimate love relationship two humans can enjoy with each other. Do you think Adam or Eve stopped liking sex after sin took over their lives? Did the way the Lord made them regarding their sexual drive stop after the fall? They did not experience a diminished sex drive or sexual desires because of their fall. They continued to enjoy sex and felt drawn to each other. What they were and what they liked before the fall was still part of their desires after the fall.

Enjoying Food

The desire for sex is no different from any other good thing the Lord had made before hell broke loose on man's soul. Genesis 3 did not eradicate the good things the Lord made, though the fall changed how man thought about and desired those things. Imagine if the Lord created food and made man dependent on food but put a distaste for food on man's palate. That does not sound like a good God. He creates things perfectly, which means food is not just for utilitarian purposes. God made food tasty so that man could enjoy it while he was storing his survival energy in his belly. He did this by giving man taste buds. Follow the formula: Man desires food. Man eats food. Man enjoys food. Man benefits from food.

It was a perfect plan. How kind of God to construct things so well. Then sin entered the world. What changed?

Nothing, in the sense that man still desires, eats, enjoys, and benefits from food. The fall did not create a different kind of man who had no connection to his pre-fallen condition. Sin did not remove man's pre-fall enjoyment of and benefit from food, but it did distort how man thought about food. He could no longer have a perfect godly experience with food. No longer was he able to desire, eat, enjoy, and benefit from food exclusively.

His newly depraved mind took good food and twisted it into a means to feed his selfish desire to indulge himself. He no longer ate food for God's glory and survival instincts (1 Corinthians 10:31). Adam and Eve's God-centered worldview turned into a dark, human-centered one. If there is a way to distort the Lord's kindness to us, we will find that way, even if we have to build a tower to Heaven to demonstrate our depravity (Genesis 11:1-9). We have the depraved ability to turn all God's blessings into personal indulgence. Food is good and meant for all to enjoy, but we are tempted to make poor food choices, including eating more than we should.

Twisted Sex

Our sex problems, like food or any kind gift from the Lord, are one of our most complicated distorted blessings from God. To scold a person for desiring sex does not help him untangle sin's distortions. To call a person evil because they make poor food choices or eat too much is just as wrongheaded. The culture will cancel you for fat shaming. Regardless of what you think about our culture's perspectives about obesity, we know that corrupting speech does not motivate a person to change; it might manipulate them for a season, but it won't motivate them for the long haul (Ephesians 4:29). To condemn a person each time he experiences temptation is like asking him to stop being human.

Rather than condemn him, it would be better to

understand how his twisted heart became that way. We know it happened, in part, due to fallenness, but there is more to the story. Your temptation may be different, but the truth is that we all experience temptation, and we have not fully conquered all our temptations. I am not condoning sinful sexual temptation or anyone who succumbs to it. I'm appealing for a more intelligent discussion about God's design for sex and our twisted desires that the fall did not eradicate. There are two extremes with some people regarding improper biblical discourse: The sexually tempted person will go to great lengths to justify their favorite kind of sinful practice. The un-tempted will uncharitably jump on any person who struggles with any sinful temptation.

No one can condone sinful sex of any kind because God does not condone it. There is no stamp to approve sinful sex, and the only acceptable kind of sex is the kind that happens between a man and a woman after they are married. The Hebrew writer could not say it more clearly:

> Let marriage be held in honor among all, and let the marriage bed be undefiled, for God will judge the sexually immoral and adulterous.
>
> (Hebrews 13:4)

Any other kind of sex places the participants under the judgment of God. Unbiblical sex is the practice of darkened and futile minds, those who live according to the spirit of this age, not under the management and empowerment of the Holy Spirit.

> They are darkened in their understanding, alienated from the life of God because of the ignorance that is in them, due to their hardness of heart. They have become callous and have given themselves up to sensuality, greedy to practice every kind of impurity.
>
> (Ephesians 4:18-19)

Post Genesis 3 Struggler

There is a difference between a person who is making excuses for their gluttony and a person who is honest about their temptation to overeat. The humble admission is what I appreciated about the comment from my old, godly friend. If a person comes to you and says they are tempted to overeat, I recommend you do not condemn them but thank them. If they have the humility and trust to let you know they are a Genesis 2 person who has been twisted by Genesis 3, encourage them to continue in dialogue as you keep watch on your heart since you're a fellow struggler too (Galatians 6:1-2; Matthew 18:33). Don't brand them like a pervert or a lesser person in the human race because they are honest about how God made them and how sin has twisted them.

Their struggle may be because impure thoughts control them. Maybe they have a specific weakness that is different from yours. It could be because something happened to them in their childhood that twisted their understanding of sex and its purposes. I do not know why they have a twisted perspective and practice of sex, but I do want to make sure they know these two things: They are experiencing something normal, which is why I want to sympathize with them (Hebrews 4:15), and I want to applaud their desire for the opposite sex. A desire for the opposite gender is God's design. To not struggle (Romans 3:10-12) or not desire the opposite sex denies the truth of God's Word.

Those who succumb to sexual temptation are not unlike the rest of us. We all have our dark battles with sin's temptations. The sexually sinful mind does not understand a gospel orientation for sex. Rather than seeing sex as for the other person, they have turned sex onto themselves. The gospel orientation for sex has the receiver in view because the gospel is always subject-to-object-focused (John 3:16). The Lord gives His gifts so others benefit from them. Sadly, we live in a post-Genesis three world, which means our temptation is to take God's blessings and turn them onto ourselves to feed and satisfy our selfish pleasures. It is the inwardly curved soul. Rather than seeing sex as a gift to give to a spouse, the sexually twisted person sees themselves as the receiver of sexual pleasure.

Call to Action

1. **THE PARENT:** Sexual temptation will be part of your child's life. He may be cute, cuddly, and oblivious right now, but he will not always be that way. Be warned and discerning about how God made him with a desire to enjoy sex, and be proactive as you think about how his fallenness will try to distort sex. Your worst move is to bury your head in the sand by thinking your child is different. No child is different when it comes to distorted sex. There is no special group of un-tempted men, no matter how godly they are or how godly you want to think they are (including your pastor). "He raised up David to be their king, of whom he testified and said, 'I have found in David the son of Jesse a man after my heart, who will do all my will.'" (Acts 13:22). "It happened, late one afternoon, when David arose from his couch and was walking on the roof of the king's house, that he saw from the roof a woman bathing; and the woman was very beautiful" (2 Samuel 11:2).

2. **THE WIFE:** Your husband is not different from the rest of us. It is wise and humble for husbands and wives to talk about these things. The gospel should have freed you by this time—assuming you are Christians (Hebrews 5:12-14). It should have you in such a place where there is nothing to hide and nothing to protect. Suppose you can't talk about your sanctification journey, specifically about this crucial aspect of it. In that case, I recommend you find help because your marriage is not as stable as it should be.

3. **THE TEMPTED:** "But each person is tempted when he is lured and enticed by his own desire. Then desire when it has conceived gives birth to sin, and sin

when it is fully grown brings forth death" (James 1:14-15). Friend, you are tempted toward bad sex, but do not be discouraged: temptation and yielding to temptation are two remarkably different things, though there is only a thin line that separates them. To tempt is an essential play from the evil ones. They know that every human has an attraction for the thing they are swinging in front of their craving hearts (James 4:1-2). If a man were not pre-wired to like the thing the evil ones were tempting him with, they would not try to tempt him with it. They only tempt you if you can succumb to the temptation.

4. **THE REST:** Something tempts everyone. Though the consequences of some sins can be more grievous than others, do not think your sin puts smaller nails in the hands of Christ (James 2:10). Only the person struggling with gospel amnesia would slam the door on a sexual struggler as though that person has a plague. We all have the plague. Yours may put you in a more acceptable category within the Christian community, but not before God; we're all filthy in His eyes (Isaiah 64:6) and stand in need of Christ's righteousness. Can you admit that you struggle with temptation? Do you see yourself as better than other people? If so, what righteous merit makes you better? We must not treat strugglers the way the Lord would never treat us when we bring our struggles to Him.

And should not you have had mercy on your fellow servant, as I had mercy on you?

(Matthew 18:33)

5

What Girls Should Know

Pornography is a pervasive sin in the sense that the outward behavior—viewing porn—speaks to a heart idolatry that is not as evident at first glance. Though there is wisdom in cutting off porn behavior (Matthew 5:29-30), the only way to be truly free is by rooting it out at its source, which implies identifying the idol that feeds the porn addiction. There will be many idols operative in a porn person's heart. You may find the idol of comfort, respect, control, power, or reputation. Though this chapter will not deal with the rooting out of these idols, it's vital for those caring for the caught individual to understand that there is more happening with the person in porn than what meets the eye.

Pervasive Porn Problem

Because porn is an external problem, you must look underneath the behavioral sin to see the pervasive nature of it. There is always at least one idol that feeds our behaviors, and it's not unusual to find the same idol manifesting in different ways. When it come to pornography, you want to be in-tune to how these idols are operational in the person's life. When his wife learns about his porn problem, she will not connect these dots for obvious reasons: the devastation will be intense and, typically, her heart sinks as her mind wonders, thinking that his problem has something to do with her.

The untethered mind might say, "I'm not satisfying him physically." Instead of thinking of his deficient and depraved life, she will begin punishing herself with thoughts about not being what he needs, which is why he chose porn. It seems counterintuitive for her to consider how this problem has nothing to do with her, but once that stronghold takes her mind captive, it's hard to break, even though the Bible could not be clearer: Nobody can cause another person to sin, no matter what the sin is (James 1:14-15). Sin is a choice. There is no permission for any husband to explain his sin away or dump it on another person, including his wife.

We're personally accountable to God for our actions. "The devil made me do it" or "my wife made me do it" won't wash with the Savior. "David said to Nathan, 'I have sinned against the LORD'" (2 Samuel 12:13), and he was right. He went on to say, "Against you, you only, have I sinned and done what is evil in your sight, so that you may be justified in your words and blameless in your judgment" (Psalm 51:4). David's heart must be every man's starting point if he wants help with his sin. The harsh truth is that the porn guy is not thinking about his wife at all, except for how he is lusting after her. It's all about his gratification. It's all about using someone—anyone—to bring sensual pleasure to himself.

Biblical Sex or Porn Sex

Addicts are users, like someone addicted to drugs. There is no way his wife could ever measure up to his sinful cravings; no wife could. For the porn guy, his wife is just another body for him to find lust-filled pleasure. He has no loyalty to anyone but himself, as though being married means nothing more than satisfying his lusts. Part of the wife's struggle is that she will be thinking about biblical sex rather than porn sex. That is why she has a hard time thinking rightly about the problem. That is why she may succumb to the temptation to believe it has something to do with her. She's thinking biblical sex while he's acting out porn sex. Those acts are two different things with two different objectives.

> The husband should give to his wife her conjugal rights, and likewise the wife to her husband. For the wife does not have authority over her own body, but the husband does. Likewise the husband does not have authority over his own body, but the wife does. Do not deprive one another, except perhaps by agreement for a limited time, that you may devote yourselves to prayer; but then come together again, so that Satan may not tempt you because of your lack of self-control.
>
> (1 Corinthians 7:3-5)

Paul was clear on what biblical sex was supposed to be. Biblical sex is always about the other person. Biblical sex is about the other-centered attitude of the gospel (Mark 10:45). Gospel-centered sex is about giving graciously to the spouse. When the wife understands this truth, she knows it would not matter who she was or what she had because it's not about her primarily. Yes, it should be about her if her husband understood and applied the gospel to his marriage, but that is not what he is doing. He is sinning, and his sin is self-centered. There is little difference in the porn guy's mind between his wife, an Internet porn star, or a prostitute. I'm speaking of the hideousness of this sin. It hardly matters who becomes the object of his lust. It's all about sinful passion. This problem is a real-world travesty that is decimating the Christian community.

It Is About You

With that said, every wife needs to know she has a sexual role in the marriage, which should emulate the gospel. If she is gospel-motivated, she will apply Paul's teaching because a biblical wife knows her body belongs to her husband (1 Corinthians 7:4). While the spouse may not be the cause of the man's choice to look at porn, she can tempt him to look at porn. This distinction is critical, and she should understand it. There are things she can do to lure him into looking elsewhere when it comes to sex. Let me share with you three of the more common ways a wife can tempt her husband toward lust.

- She can disrespect him by complaining, nagging, demeaning, or withholding encouragement. Men are not as strong and unfazed as they may want you to believe. Men can be real babies, including me, when it comes to craving respect. It is part of our identity. We want people to appreciate us, especially for what we do. Our Adamic wiring is from the Lord. Doing stuff and taking care of things is how God made us. A wife who does not understand this and withholds her respect and admiration from her husband can tempt him to desire appreciation from other places and other people.
- Withholding sex is a big no-no in marriage, too. This warning was from Paul. One of the best ways a wife can show her admiration and love for her husband is by wanting him physically. This desire to want to be wanted is another weak area for guys. They want to be wanted sexually by their wives. A wife who wants to be intimate with her husband is honoring him.
- Many women do duty sex because of the conflict in their marriages. They reluctantly honor Paul's request not to withhold, but they don't engage their

mates in the moment of physical intimacy. They hope that he will experience satisfaction soon so that it will be over. Soon. She is sending a clear statement to the husband that she does not desire him, and that can become a source of temptation.

I realize many wives reading this are frustrated women. When I write about how things ought to be, some of them respond in anger. No doubt what I've written here will be a source of frustration to many women who feel trapped in marriages that seem to have no hope of changing. To talk about their failing marriage would be beyond the scope of this book. This chapter is for those ladies who want to marry a guy but do not understand the comprehensive complexities of porn. I hope that many soon-to-be-married ladies will read this chapter, and it will help them avoid future pitfalls. If your marriage is already in the pit, you need help in other ways. However, there are truths here that you will have to interact with at some point if you want a changed marriage.

Salvation Is Not Enough

To put off your old self, which belongs to your former manner of life and is corrupt through deceitful desires.

(Ephesians 4:22)

Some people believe that all you need is salvation to overcome a porn addiction. I wish that were the case, but it's not. The issue is more complex, and Paul provides us with a clue when he talks about our former manner of life. For example, the majority of people who get into porn get into porn before God regenerates them (Galatians 6:1-2). Though God saved them at a young age, they were not fortified or equipped to understand and resist porn. Maybe it was imposed upon them by a knucklehead friend.

Perhaps they stumbled upon it. A typical statement that I hear from older guys after they come out of porn is they were not honest with their future wives about it. They also were not transparent with others. Porn is a secret sin.

These single guys may tell their soon-to-be wives they looked at porn, which most guys have to admit because of the ubiquitous reality of it, but they withhold some of the facts, especially if it's still a struggle. The girlfriend is satisfied with his humble acknowledgment, and they move on with their relationship. Ten to fifteen years later, she catches him in porn. What I have just described is the most common scenario for porn in marriage. It would behoove any young lady to be more inquisitive, though I think many of them do not want to know, especially after the engagement and just before the imminent wedding. Here are a few probing questions any young couple should be willing to work through as it relates to pornography. These questions are explicit and only intended for the couple on the verge of marriage, not for any random dating couple who is not serious about or strategically planning on marrying each other.

1. Have you ever looked at porn?
2. How much porn have you viewed?
3. How often did you look at porn?
4. What were some of the ways you enjoyed porn?
5. Why did you do it?
6. Who knew about it?
7. Who did you seek to help you?
8. When was the last time you masturbated?
9. Why did you masturbate?
10. How often have you masturbated this past year? The past five years?
11. What accountability measures do you have in your life to help you work through pornography and masturbation?

Questions #6, #7, and #11 will reveal to you how honest he is because it is rare for a person to defeat porn alone. It would be questionable if he said he overcame porn temptations without anyone knowing about it. If he humbly sought help from a spiritual mentor, you can know he has been thinking rightly about the problem and what it takes to overcome it. If you talked to the person who helped him, that would be instructive and reassuring to you. People will always seek to put their best foot forward. When it comes to porn, you do not want to take a guy's word alone. There is too much at stake. If you can talk to another person and get their insight, that would be wise. If your boyfriend is humble, he would be more than willing to tell you all you want to know. The humble person has nothing to protect and nothing to hide. Your questions and his answers will tell you quickly who you are dealing with and where he stands with God and you. If he becomes angry, defensive, or evasive, it's "on you" if you marry him.

A Former Manner of Life

Everyone has a former manner of life. We're born in sin, and because of adverse shaping influences and poor personal choices, sin gloms onto our lives before we encounter the Savior. There are no exceptions, making it vital that we do not self-righteously condemn another fellow sinner, especially when their sin is not as socially acceptable as ours. In one sense, all sin is the same in that any transgression, no matter how big or small, will put Christ on Adam's tree. "For whoever keeps the whole law but fails in one point has become guilty of all of it" (James 2:10). The murderer and the gossiper are the same in that they both have sinned. Note how Paul does not make a distinction between a murderer and a person who sins with her tongue. There is one category: we're guilty before God.

They were filled with all manner of unrighteousness, evil, covetousness, malice. They are full of envy, murder, strife, deceit, maliciousness. They are gossips, slanderers, haters of God, insolent, haughty, boastful, inventors of evil, disobedient to parents, foolish, faithless, heartless, ruthless.

(Romans 1:29-31)

We know that some sins are weightier and have different consequences. But there is no contradiction here. It is two truths about our sinfulness. In one way, all sin is the same. In another way, they are not; the consequences for some sins can be severe. Regardless, the truth is that we all have our sins, and hopefully, we are agonizing before God, seeking His help as well as the help of others so we can overcome our sinfulness. It is common for a brother to struggle with porn. It is common for a sister to wrestle with beauty insecurities. Both of them are the same in that they are mocking Christ by seeking satisfaction outside of His gospel-filled provision. Sinning, as a saint, is more natural than one might think.

Don't Forget Caught Brothers

Brothers, if anyone is caught in any transgression, you who are spiritual should restore him in a spirit of gentleness. Keep watch on yourself, lest you too be tempted. Bear one another's burdens, and so fulfill the law of Christ.

(Galatians 6:1-2)

There is one more dynamic to this conversation that I want to insert, which is the Galatians 6:1-2 factor. Paul is talking about addiction here. It is possible for a young man to be addicted to porn or, to use Paul's language, to be caught in any transgression. There are millions of Christians caught in sin today. For example, there are women stuck in anxiety, unforgiveness, and bitterness. And sin has captured men in porn and drugs. There are men and women trapped in the bondage of identity issues: the man regarding his work and the woman about her appearance.

We are addictive people, and it's common to become caught in sin. We should not be surprised by this because that was the purpose of Christ's coming: to save us from ourselves. Sin is destructive and does not discriminate. Satan has one objective: to kill and devour, and being a Christian does not automatically insulate you from his devices. (See John 10:10; 1 Peter 5:8.) We can be a mess at times, but we do not have to be discouraged. Christ has overcome the world (John 16:33). With a little wisdom, faith, perseverance, and a few insightful questions, you will be well-equipped to move forward into marriage.

Call to Action

1. How would you help a wife break the stronghold of thinking her husband's porn problem is because of her?

2. How would you help her to see that she may have fueled his temptations, even though she is not the cause?

3. Why is it crucial for a girlfriend to know about a guy's sin history with porn?

4. How would you help her resist self-righteousness should she find out her boyfriend or spouse struggles with porn?

6

Your Boyfriend's Temptation

Strangers marry each other, and whoever you marry, you marry all of them, including their mind. Though you trust God with your future marriage partner and hope for the best, you know there is an element of mystery about how things will go because you will never be 100% aware of who your marriage partner is. Though it sounds pessimistic, it is a recognition of your finitude and your responsibility to ensure that your dating relationship is a sober opportunity for clear-headed decision-making and courageous choices. For the girl, she must understand sexual temptation, specifically how it has affected her boyfriend. As my friend, Mable, was thinking about these things, she wrote me the following letter.

Boyfriend Questions

Recently, I finished your book, "So, You Want To Get Married?" It has opened my eyes to a few things I had not considered. You answered a lot of my questions and gave me clear direction on how to think about guys and porn, but more specifically about the struggles (or potential struggles) of my fiancé. I feel better equipped to serve him as a helper after we get married. With that said, you also stirred up a few questions, and I wanted to know if you could answer them for me. After going through some of the things you suggested, I wondered if some of my questions would be too personal to ask now. Here are the ones we have discussed already.

1. *Have you ever looked at porn?*
2. *How much porn did you view?*
3. *How often did you look at porn?*
4. *What were some of the ways you used porn?*
5. *Why did you do it?*
6. *Who knew about it?*
7. *Who did you seek for help?*

These discussions were great, and my boyfriend seemed open about his past struggles. However, there were a few other questions that I wanted to ask but was afraid to.

8. *When was the last time you masturbated?*
9. *Why did you masturbate?*
10. *How often have you masturbated this past year? ...the past five years?*
11. *What accountability measures do you have in your life to help you work through sexual temptation?*

I would also like to know if there are any physical signs or attitudes a guy who is secretly in porn may exhibit that a girl can perceive? Is there a difference between struggling with lust—with seeing girls dressed immodestly or in the media—versus struggling with porn? Lastly, would you agree that there is a difference between a short struggle with porn versus a multi-year addiction for a Christian? Repentance characterizes a true believer. Sin no longer describes believers because 1 Corinthians 6:9-11 says that "such were some of you, but you were washed." It seems to me that some sins should no longer be a regular, habitual part of a Christian's life because he can repent. Wouldn't it be true that a man who claims to know the Lord but has a multi-year addiction to porn and hasn't overcome it probably does not know the Lord?

Let's Get Personal

Your questions are fantastic, though they are over-the-top for most Christians because of the explicit nature of them. In the counseling world, we deal with these things regularly, so they are not off-putting to me, but essential things for couples who are about to get married to discuss. I have dealt with these things for decades, nearly on a weekly basis. Sexual temptation is on a short list of the most common problems in which we all struggle. Putting my vocation aside for the moment, I do not see them as too personal as much as I see them as loving, self-protective questions. The more you care for someone, the deeper and more personal your questions should be for the person you love.

The more bound you are to a person, the more you need scrutiny regarding your long-term well-being. Jesus may have been reluctant to get up in the Pharisees' business (John 2:24-25), but He was not timid or hesitant with those who were closest to Him (Matthew 16:23). If a girl is thinking about committing the rest of her life to a guy, your questions are necessary—appropriately asked at the appropriate time. Discretion is a virtue. Perhaps you could think about your questions this way: which would be worse: to ask personal questions before your wedding day or to be devastated ten years into your marriage after you find out he has a sexual addiction?

I appreciate your caution and concern. The adult world—especially the darker side of it—should cause a cautious and wise posture that you must consider. I'm thankful you have not experienced exposure to some of the seedier things in our culture. Thus, I recommend that you ask the Spirit to give you the thought-filled illuminations and empowering grace you will need as you launch into the longest and most challenging time of your life. Though I don't want to put your future marriage on par with buying a car, please allow me to use an illustration.

Wise Due Diligence

When purchasing a car, a wise person would not hold back from asking all the right questions. She researches, investigates, makes comparisons, and asks the hard things. Why? She is about to make a significant commitment. How much more wisdom and courage do you need when thinking about your marriage? It is common for many marriages that go off the rails to miss out on these essential discussions while they are dating. Of course, I don't recommend these types of questions until there is marriage talk and strategic planning. When first dating, they are too soon and inappropriate. After marriage, you might regret the lack of due diligence.

More than likely, your first seven questions will tell you what you need to know, providing insight into your more personal ones about masturbation, addiction, and repentance. A man who looks at porn more than once has probably masturbated. It would be exceptional if that were not the case. If he has looked at porn and is honest with you about what he has done, go ahead and assume he has masturbated. Don't bury your idealistic head in the sand. If he has sought help, you can ask him if you can talk to the person who helped him so you can gain a third party's perspective. I would recommend you take an older lady with you if you do pursue his accountability partner.

If your boyfriend is humble, open, and honest, he has nothing to hide and nothing to protect. A gospel-centered worldview motivates him to live in the freedom and power of God's opinion of him, empowering him to fight the temptation to hide his sins or protect his reputation. Free men are free. They are not habitually bound, insecure, or easily offended. If he doesn't let you speak into his life at this level at this time while dating, consider it a red flag. It's during the dating relationship that a guy will be most open and conciliatory because he wants to "get the girl." If he's not, he will be even less so after you marry him.

Signs and Attitudes

One of the most common complaints I hear in marriage counseling is a husband's unwillingness to let his wife probe into his life. These husbands resist openness, honesty, and transparency. If you are planning to marry this guy, and if he resists your questions while dating, consider his response a precursor to your future marriage experience. It would be fair to multiply his replies to you—whether good or bad—by ten after you are married. Our good or bad behaviors will only increase after marriage. Only repentance can change a sinful trajectory. Dating is the wonderful, charmed, fun, romantic, put-your-best-foot-forward, but somewhat artificial season, where you do not see the truest colors of each other.

While you may have had arguments and disappointments during the dating season, whatever has happened will pale in comparison to a 24/7, uninterrupted bond that will only break at death. The first sign you should look for is his openness to your questions. He should not tell every sordid detail of his thought life, and you should not share yours either. I'm speaking more about a willingness toward humility, transparency, and honesty, not a fool who reveals his entire mind to someone. His desire and attitude to be open with you will tell you nearly all you need to know, though there are other things you will need to discern.

For example, how close to the edge does he walk

regarding sexual things? Paul told us to flee youthful lusts (2 Timothy 2:22). Which direction does he lean regarding lust? Does he run toward or away from it? "Keep your way far from her, and do not go near the door of her house" (Proverbs 5:8). The language of Scripture is severe, strong, and clear when it comes to lust. You don't go there. If a person likes living on the edge, you should perceive it and not go with him.

Study Your Man

Here are a few things you can look for as far as signs and attitudes:

- What kind of language does he use? Does he use sexual language? Flirty language? Sexually tempting language? Sexually crude language? Does he use sexual illustrations when describing things?
- How does he treat you? How does he treat his mother? How does he treat his sisters, if he has any? You're trying to discern how he treats women, especially those who have been the closest to him. You will be the closest woman to him in marriage.
- Where does he touch you? Does he protect you and your body?
- Does he look at the opposite sex in ways that seem inappropriate? Do his eyes follow a lady as she walks into a room? Can he be easily distracted by the opposite sex?
- Does he have a problem watching R-rated movies, the ones that have sexual content in them? Does he think proactively when it comes to movies? Does he quickly look away when sexual images are in front of him?
- Does he talk to you about his temptations? Is he open about his weaknesses in an appropriate way

for communicating such things? Does he ask you to help him guard his heart—to pray for him? As you go deeper into the relationship, he should be more honest with you. If not, you will be easily tempted to fornicate.

- Is he modest with what he wears? Does he want you to dress modestly?

Smoke and Fire

You asked, "Is there a difference between struggling with lust—with seeing girls dressed immodestly or in the media—versus struggling with pornography?" The answer is "Yes" and "No." There is an obvious difference, but the better question is, "What's the relationship between these two actions?" As you reflect on the previous two sections about "signs and attitudes" and "study your man," you should be able to discern if looking at girls and media are the appetizers to the main event. If he does not struggle with or if he responds in a mature way to the cultural temptations of immodesty, there is a good chance he does not struggle with pornography.

> Can a man carry fire next to his chest and his clothes not be burned? Or can one walk on hot coals and his feet not be scorched?
>
> (Proverbs 6:27-28)

My mother used to say, "Where there is smoke, there is fire." It applies here. If he struggles with the signs and attitudes, you have a problem. While there is a difference between cultural temptations and porn, cultural temptations are often the precursor to the more destructive sin pattern of porn. We understand David lived in unrepentant sin for at least a year before Nathan confronted him. (Bathsheba had already given birth to their son.) We also know he was under deep conviction from the Lord. (See Psalm 32:1-4.) There is not a strong case in Scripture for the backsliding Christian. The mantra often used by people who "got saved at five but walked away from the Lord, and now they are thirty-five and repenting" is problematic. One of the few testimonies we have of a person who walked away from the Lord in Scripture is David, and this is what he said about that season of his life:

> For when I kept silent, my bones wasted away through my groaning all day long. For day and night your hand was heavy upon me; my strength was dried up as by the heat of summer.
> (Psalm 32:3-4)

I'm not sure how you can walk away from the Lord for thirty years and experience what David experienced. With that said, I can make an argument for a person caught in an addiction and still be a Christian. I've seen it too many times not to believe this. I have counseled a few addicted people, and I do not believe all of them were unbelievers. I'm talking about individuals with a multi-decade addiction. Paul's language in Galatians 6:1 seems to support this. "Brothers, if anyone is caught in any transgression, you who are spiritual should restore him in a spirit of gentleness." The word caught is the Bible word for addiction. You referenced 1 Corinthians 6:9-11, which is a good text but not a solid one for this discussion. The general idea in Corinthians is the person who is a blatant rebel against God—a person who doesn't care about God—a reviler.

What's His Attitude

Based on all the texts that speak to sinning Christians, you can't make a case that a habitual sinner is automatically an unbeliever. There are many Christians who bring addictive lifestyles into their relationship with God (Ephesians 4:22), and sometimes it takes years for them to overcome. Think about the woman who worries all the time. Is she a Christian? What about the person who overeats and uses food as an escape when life becomes challenging? I realize from a consequential perspective that worrying is not as devastating to a person's relationships, but it can be a habitual, life-dominating sin pattern.

I don't want to happy-talk a person with a sexual sin addiction into heaven, but I also don't want to automatically say that a person with a deeply-trenched former manner of life is not a Christian. I realize I'm walking a thin line where subjectivity is present. The key you are looking for is a person's attitude about their sin. Are they humble, honest, open, transparent, and seeking help? Or are they hiding, defiant, and reviling the Word of God? The first group could be Christians, while the latter group probably is not.

Call to Action

1. What have been your parent's observations about him? I'm assuming your parents are believers and have mature, biblical wisdom. If they do not have these qualities, please discuss these things with a mature older woman in your church.
2. If you have a sister, what are her thoughts about him? Again, the assumption is she has common sense and can intuit a person, even if she does not have all the proper biblical categories.
3. Consider asking your pastor (or another spiritual leader) their thoughts about him.
4. What has been his dating/sensual history? Serial dater? One and done? Somewhere in-between? Does he need to get married, or is he trusting the Lord to bring the right person to him?
5. What do you believe the Lord is guiding you to do now?

7

Please Lust After Me

Lust does not mysteriously appear in the heart of a teenager as though it came from nowhere. Teens are like the rest of us. Lust is part of their Adamic wiring, a sobering call for every parent to cooperate with God in shaping a child's heart and life to a purer desire that is in Christ alone. This call is more than academic; the parent must model their message, giving their child a living illustration of God's love to another person. Let me illustrate this point by sharing the fictional account of Biffina that shines a light on a real-world problem that is not fictional in too many of our young people's lives.

Letter From Biffina

Hi, my name is Biffina. I'm 22 years old. For as long as I can remember, I've wanted guys to like me. It makes me feel good to catch the eye of a guy. I realize men are weak; the perfect opportunity for an adrenaline rush to manipulate them with my looks. Honestly, I don't want to sleep with any of them or even date them. They're perverts. Okay, maybe I would like to have sex with a couple of them, but it's mostly about getting their attention. I like the power when I catch them watching me. It's like fifteen minutes of fame in a fantastical way.

I was in Starbucks the other day, and there was this guy with his wife. (I think it was his wife.) She did not see me because her back was to me, but he was facing me. The whole time he was talking to his wife, he was scoping me out. If we were alone, I would have left because he gave me the creeps. I'm so glad he was with his wife and could only sneak looks. (I'd hate to be her.) I owned that dude. He was under my spell, and it felt good. I suspect if this creep knew how I was manipulating him, he would be ticked (or maybe embarrassed). Then again, he may be delusional, thinking I was interested, or so perverted that he doesn't care. We both were getting our fix on in Starbucks. I teased him. He took a thirty-minute spin into his fantasy world. We go our merry way.

The Path to Lust

When I was a child, I used to idolize my dad. He had a strong personality and seemed to know everything. There was no doubt he ruled the roost. Mom never talked back to him, and the little chickadees toed the line. Dad was our angry ruler of the roost. By the time I became a teen, the selfishness and anger my dad had for Mom began to spill over on me. I didn't know how to process it at first. I always assumed he was right and that what he did to Mom was their deal, not mine. Then he got mad at me, though I did not connect the dots initially.

It was during my teenage years when it occurred to me it was his problem, not mine. I always assumed I was wrong when he yelled at me. "I am the problem." What does a punk kid like me know anyhow? After I became a teen, I learned it was not always my fault, my brother's, or my mom's. It took me a long time to get here, but I did learn eventually: My dad is an angry, selfish man. He didn't love me; he didn't love anyone but himself.

He was a pompous, self-absorbed jerk who expected everything to go his way, and if it didn't, he would go off on us. It all came to a head when I was fifteen. That's when I realized I was cute, had the right kind of body, and boys liked me. It is hard for me to explain how good it feels to know I am not as bad as my dad made me feel. It was like, "Finally! Somebody liked me!"

The Lust Rules

I would spend about an hour getting ready for school. I always made sure my shorts were just short enough and my panty lines showed through. I learned that trick from my sister. She was a senior when I hit high school. We bonded quickly, and she taught me the rules of lust—as we liked to call them. She told me how guys preferred to leave things to the imagination. "Never show it all, Sis. Only give them enough to where they can fill in the rest." That was her motto. There were some things we did in school that would give my dad a coronary if he knew—but he never knew, which is one of the upsides to having a self-absorbed, emotionally detached father.

He kept his head stuck up his reputation so much that he was blind to what was going on with us. He thought he was on top of things. He was only on top of his image. As long as I went to church, said all the right things, and made A's in school, he left me alone— for the most part. I made him look good; I checked the boxes that kept his reputation intact and lived the way I wanted to.
Score!
Biffina

Your Approval Drive

Biffina's story is pure fiction. But not really. At Life Over Coffee, we can monitor the search criteria of people who are looking for content on our site. Though we cannot tell who the individuals are, we can know what they are looking for by their search criteria. It helps me to know what to write about if I know what folks are looking for. Recently, I was scrolling through a few searches and noticed there were a lot of people using search criteria that began with "How to." One of those "How to" searches was "How to get guys to lust after me." Initially, I laughed, but as I continued to reflect on this person's search, my knee-jerk reaction turned sad. I was not shocked by what I saw. This person is representative of millions of women who enjoy the pleasure of a guy's lustful gaze. She represents what is at the heart of broken humanity, which is not gender exclusive; men like women noticing them, too.

There is something inside of us that wants to be appreciated, accepted, loved, and respected by others. We were born this way because God put those desires in our hearts (Genesis 1:27; 1 John 4:8; 2 Timothy 2:15). Being made in the image of God comes with the hardwired desire to be loved, which was fully satisfied at the dawn of time when a perfect Being made perfectly contented people. Adam and Eve experienced the sinless reciprocal love between each other and their Creator. Then their dawn turned dark, and everything blew sideways. Satan threw the first family a curve ball when he dramatically took control of their approval drives. What used to be satisfied by sinless means could now be met by evil manipulations. Desires became depraved, and the man and woman could exercise a new up-fitted power that scratched their ungodly cravings for love, approval, significance, and acceptance.

> But each person is tempted when he is lured and
> enticed by his own desire.
>
> (James 1:14)

A Fatal Flaw

*Almighty God, you have made us for yourself, and our
hearts are restless till they find their rest in you, so lead
us by your Spirit so that in this life we may live to your
glory and in the life to enjoy you forever.*

– Augustine

What God meant for good for all humanity, the devil meant
for evil (Genesis 50:20; Romans 5:12). The objects of our
affection changed after our first parents succumbed to sin,
and our desire for love fell prey to the distorting effects
of sin. Biffina is a case study of a person born with an
Adamic deficit who sinfully craves approval, significance,
acceptance, and affection. She has yet to come to the
regenerating place of finding those things in God (John
3:7), and to make matters worse, her dad compounded
her preexisting Adamic condition. One of two things will
happen to Biffina: She will find God despite her dad, or she
will continue on the same self-centered path as her dad. He
gave her a fantastic education. He made sure she attended
the right church. He legislated excellence in every way.
If the world were producing children, his children would
be the prototypes. But there was a proverbial fly in his
parenting methodological ointment—two to be exact: He
refused to factor in the spiritual dynamics of her heart, and
his self-absorption fed and motivated her Adamic desire for
serial lusting.

Exporting Lust to Children

You can give a child all the accouterments of the world, but if you don't spiritually shepherd their hearts toward the Lord, all your efforts will more than likely blow up in your face. Biffina's strongest desire is to be emotionally connected by love to someone—to anyone—and she does not know how "God alone" is the fulfillment of those desires. Her dad was the gatekeeper of her soul. He had the opportunity to cooperate with God in directing her heart to the Lord by his other-centered example or tempt her to go the way of the world. By the time she was twelve, the Adamic possibilities of the world had captured her heart.

Too often, parents who miss this important opportunity to help their children down a righteous path do not understand how their own lukewarm (or non-existent) spiritual relationship with Christ impacts the children they are supposed to guide. You cannot export to your children what you don't possess. Biffina's dad did not have an authentic walk with God, which disqualified him from helping her have one. What he did export to her was what was in his heart: self-centeredness, self-absorption, and self-actualization, which motivated her to reject both him and God. Hypocrisy does not play well with Christianity; it ruins families.

It is one thing for an unbeliever to deny God. They do it because they do not believe it works. What would you expect them to do? But it is profoundly sad when Christianized children with Christianized parents reject Christ. These kids do so because they have seen objective proof that it's a hoax, as they have observed their hypocritical parents. If parents put forth Christianity as the way, but Christianity does not authentically grip and affect them, there is a good chance their children will reject Christianity. If they do come to Christ at all, it will be despite of the parent's parenting, which usually happens after the children leave home.

Call to Action

1. The first and foremost thing to address when it comes to shaping the heart of a child is our motive for living the life that we live. What do you believe Biffina's dad's rationale was for associating with Christianity? What was the primary motive that shaped his life? What should he do differently?

The good news is that God does not hide what our motives for serving Him should be. Exodus 20:3 is one clear example of this, as we are told to put no other gods before the Sovereign Lord. Matthew 22:37 is another place where Jesus said loving the Lord more than anything else must be preeminent in our hearts (Colossians 1:18). He went on to say in Luke 14:26 that all love, when compared to our love for God, should look like hate. There is no mystery here. If we want to be part of what God can do in our children's lives, specifically as it pertains to their sensuality and desires for love, the place to begin is in our hearts. Here are a few more questions that may help you reflect upon your heart's motivations for participating in Christianity.

2. What have been your thoughts about God today? How has your love of Christ been displayed throughout your life today?
3. What is something you hope people do not find out about you? What is something that you cherish more than Christ (Matthew 6:21)? What does that thing say about your relationship with Him?

It may benefit you to share your thoughts with a friend. Two of the more beautiful things about Christianity are that we enjoy our life with Christ in a community and that we can always have a do-over. The world tries to evolve to a better self-made image through behavioral modification strategies and techniques. Christians are transformed into the image of Jesus Christ (2 Corinthians 3:18), as the Word of God (James 1:22) and the Spirit of God have their way in our hearts (Ephesians 4:30; 1 Thessalonians 5:19).

4. Will you be honest about where you are with God? Will you be open about your secret desires and ongoing frustrations? Who will you share these things with?

Perhaps you have blown it with your child. Do not be discouraged. It's not too late to change (Psalm 32:1-3). No matter what you have done wrong, God can bring good out of it. Grace has broad borders for people who are prone to wander. You can be part of your child's God-centered solution. Keep in mind that children don't insulate themselves from the lusts of the world. They were born with sinful desires in their hearts. They are not isolated from the attitudes, words, and behaviors of their parents. The battle against your child's cravings begins in your heart, not theirs, and it's your family community context that is the most prominent redemptive influence in this fight. Will you help your child to set her affections on Jesus? Start with the questions that I have asked in this call to action. Share your responses with a friend, and then begin mapping a plan to cooperate with God in the restoration of your child.

8

Wives and Cyber Women

Social media is ubiquitous, and there are many redemptive applications of it. At Life Over Coffee, we talk about the redemptive uses of technology as we ponder how to use this common grace mercy for God's fame. But with all good things, there is always the insipid Adamic smell of death that lures people into the darker side of what should be a means of grace. Social media has many untoward temptations; one of those is the comparison trap that stirs a desire to compete with the culture's view of appearance, attractiveness, acceptance, and approval. Many women succumb to this temptation, especially as they age. As one wife asked me, "How do I compete with cyber women as my body continues to waste away?"

Distraught Wife

I don't watch porn, but I know my husband has viewed it frequently. Even television bombards my mind with its version of the perfect woman. I struggle with being insecure already, but it becomes worse when I think about how I compete with the ladies on the Internet who are always tens. The little bit I have seen of these women makes me realize there is no way I can compete with them.

What am I to do with these thoughts? They are like a mental stronghold. Whenever my husband becomes angry with me, the thought goes through my mind that he will bolt for another woman if I don't meet his needs. Even if he does not bolt, I know he satisfies himself with those cyber ladies who are in a league of their own. What am I to do?

–Distraught Wife

Many Christian women are in a seemingly impossible situation. The external pressure from movies and television is pumped into their minds 24/7, telling them what is perfect. The dream weavers in the entertainment industry have all the tools to deliver titillating and tantalizing candy to the male ego. Then there is the pressure of porn because it is a significant and satisfying player in the male fantasy world. The fantasy is why the pursuer of the cyberwoman does not have to catch a real one. Imagine that! It's the imagination that makes porn so perfect for the depraved mind. All a guy has to do is look at the perfect woman through the lens of the Internet while enjoying her with his mind's eye. It is not about being with her. It is about the theater of his mind, which is full of thoughts as he plays the hero in his cyber-role play.

Perfect Competition

The Christian wife cannot compete with this kind of assault on her marriage. The cards are stacked against her because she could never win him if her strategy were to compete with perfect competition. What could she do anyway? How would she enter the competition, even if it were possible? The testimony of the Word of God says none of us can compete with perfection, which is the purpose of the gospel: to come and transform incomplete, broken, and imperfect people. To attempt to become the ideal through self-generated efforts is a fool's mission. It is biblical legalism—the relationship-killing process of trying to merit the affection of another person through self-reliant, self-effort.

Whether you seek to earn God's love or your man's love, you will not secure or sustain it through self-sufficient means. Biblical love is a gift given, not a gift demanded or earned. To secure and sustain perfected beauty and physicality is impossible. Even cyberwomen cannot do this. They eventually become old material and are discarded as cyber dust. Their shelf life is a narrow window of opportunity, and once they can no longer meet the criteria necessary, the newer cyber version replaces them. The impossibility of sustained perfection is why it is delusional to go down that road.

- The Christian wife cannot be perfect in beauty or physicality.
- The porn woman cannot be perfect in beauty or physicality.

A Better Way

There is a better way to think about this problem of competing against perfection. The first place to begin is with a sober-minded shift in worldviews. Lucia told me while we were dating, "Guys date the girl in the sports car, but marry the girl in the Festiva." (A Ford Festiva is a glorified golf cart. Think about a golf cart with doors. That is what Lucia had when we were dating.) I am unsure if she had statistical data to support her claim, but I loved her perspective, plus the possibility of not having to purchase an expensive car should we tie the knot. Dating the hot babe in a sports car may be fun, but it is a relationship you want to give to many prayers and supplications if you plan to marry her. Dating a girl in a glorified golf cart has long-term potential without breaking the bank or the bond.

Lucia's lack of showiness is one of the many things that made her appealing. I knew she would be easy to please, and because my handsomeness was somewhat lacking, I felt as though we could make a go of it. Imagine being married to a woman who had to have the perfect home, the newest car, and the latest fashions. The needle on her satisfaction meter would always be pointed to a ten, which means her happiness would rise or fall, depending on her husband's ability to deliver those uninterrupted tens. The man who must have a hot babe puts the same pressure on his wife. It is a trap that will kill any marriage. If the only type of beauty that matters is external, the relationship is doomed.

> Do not let your adorning be external—the braiding of hair and the putting on of gold jewelry, or the clothing you wear—but let your adorning be the hidden person of the heart with the imperishable beauty of a gentle and quiet spirit, which in God's sight is very precious.
>
> (1 Peter 3:3-4)

Who Are You?

Perhaps you are a woman with imperishable beauty (or at least you're striving toward it), but your husband is looking for something more external. Let me burst that balloon for you, and my goal is not to be harsh but to move the conversation into reality rather than a delusional state: your relationship will never glorify God until he changes. What are your choices? There are two: try to be what he believes is beautiful, maintain it for the rest of your marriage, or work on your imperishable beauty while trusting God to change your husband's idolatrous heart. I am not advocating being out of shape and letting yourself go physically. That is as unwise as it is unbiblical.

I am appealing to you to be rational, reasonable,

moderate, and disciplined, but not a fifty-something who is more concerned about how you look on the outside than who you are on the inside. Think about it this way: If you try to compete with cyber women to make your husband happy, you will have to become something like a cyber woman. Perchance, you could accomplish this feat; all you would gain is a man who uses you to satisfy his lusts. His fascination with perfected beauty is not about love but unrestrained lust. Would it make you feel better to have your husband lusting after you rather than lusting after other women? Some wives would say "yes" to this, and I understand the impulse, but is that the kind of marriage you want? If it is, you do not have a marriage. You have a mutual need-meeting negotiation:

- Husband says, "I will love you as long as you look a certain way."
- Wife says, "I will look a certain way as long as you love me."

The Cyber Wife

Beautiful women, nice toys, and drugs have one thing in common: they are idols of the lust-depraved heart. To compete with the cyber woman is to be a cyber woman. To give your husband his perfect, beautified image of a woman to make him happy is similar to appeasing a child who is throwing a tantrum, demanding you acquiesce to his infantile babbling. Give him his toy, and he will be satisfied. It is similar to giving a crack addict another bump to take another trip. As long as he can get his fix, he will be happy. The answer is not to see how obese and ugly you can become, and it's not to see how beautiful or perfect you can become. The answer is how you relate to God as a married woman regardless of whether your husband follows you in your pursuit of holiness (1 Corinthians 11:1).

- If he does not follow you as you follow Christ, you will not have a husband or a marriage that will glorify God in the way he and it should.
- If you fall into the competition trap, then an immature husband and an unsatisfied wife will not glorify God either.

The first thing you will have to do is address your heart. You will have to change (if thinking about the competition manages your mind, creating a thought fortress that holds you captive). Since your spouse is not listening or asking for help, but you are, begin with yourself. You will have to come to a place where you do not need your husband's approval, acceptance, or affection. You will also have to lose your fear of losing him. If he is already looking at porn, you do not have him anyway. You are merely one of his porn women, just not the one he wants.

A Dating Aside

TO ALL GIRLFRIENDS: You can run away if lust has trapped your boyfriend (2 Timothy 2:22). Break up while you have a chance (or you better make sure you both are getting help.) It is straightforward to discern where your boyfriend is regarding these things by how he treats you. You are in a good spot if he is more interested in your sanctification than your beauty. If he is not leading you spiritually, you better pause and reflect on your relationship. By all means, seek biblical wisdom and counsel. If you have to win him with your beauty, you will lose him shortly after marriage. Beauty is skin deep, and if that is the depth of your boyfriend's thoughts about you, nobody can compete with that fantasy. Eventually, he will discard and replace you, though he may stay in the marriage. Follow the advice of God's Word rather than the mandates of our culture: Beauty is vain. Do not try to keep up with culture's temptations.

Charm is deceitful, and beauty is vain, but a woman who fears the Lord is to be praised.

(Proverbs 31:30)

Suffering's Choice

One of the hardest things for a woman who feels the need to compete with cyberwomen is to realize the actual condition of her marriage. Though it is a cold and harsh reality, she must accept the truth about what is happening with them. Disbelief regarding reality will hinder anyone from getting to where they need to be in their journey with God and others. As you begin to accept the reality of your marriage, you will have to guard your heart against anger, bitterness, unforgiveness, resentfulness, and regret. You will also have to protect against retaliating toward your husband or becoming angry at God. There will be a temptation to sin.

None of these things will honor God or make His name great. They will also hinder you from accomplishing your heart's desire: to win your husband's affection, restore your marriage, and magnify the name of God (Psalm 34:3). Being mean and snarky toward your husband will not win him to God. Do not be that wife. If you have followed these ideas closely, you have discerned how you are up against two impossible situations; it does not matter which way you go; the path will be hard and hurtful. If you try to compete with cyber women, you will eventually realize its impossibility. If you set aside your desires while seeking to win your husband to Christ, you will also suffer.

The difference between the first and second options is that the Lord is not against you if you pursue setting aside your desires for His fame, regardless of the outcome. He gives empowering favor to anyone who chooses His path of suffering versus the world's path of suffering (James 4:6). He will oppose you if you try to win your husband by replacing the cyber women with your version of cultural beauty. That is not winning your husband. It is switching his drug from them to you. Christians do not compete with the world. We are set apart from the world, and if the world does not want to follow our lead—including your husband— it is their loss and our cross to bear.

Call to Action

1. What do you fear that compels you to think you must compete with cyber women?
2. What insecurities do you need to address that will release you from your husband's sin?
3. How do you need to mature in the imperishable beauty God offers?
4. What would hinder you from talking with someone who could help your husband? What about talking to someone who can assist you? Will you chat with someone soon?

9

Exporting Modesty

Typically, when people think about modesty, their minds immediately go to what a person wears and arbitrary preferences rather than the heart's motivations that influence their external choices. Perhaps when I mention "modesty," your impulse was similar: "Great, he will tell us what to wear!" If so, you're normal. But my goal here is different from mandating universal clothing stipulations. I am not going to suggest what you should wear. I want to focus on something more vital—our hearts, the genesis of all of our thoughts, attitudes, words, and behaviors, including how we adorn our bodies.

Heart Matters

Wearing clothes is about as every day as it gets. From two to twelve years of age, a child will put on clothes approximately 4000 times. Parents have a dozen or so years to teach their children how to connect a modest Christian worldview to their daily lives. Teaching modesty is our always-recurring opportunity to envision children. Imagine if we learn a new habit in twenty-one days, how much more our children will have entrenched thinking about modesty—for good or evil—long before becoming teens. But like all our behaviors, learning modesty begins in our hearts, not on our backs. What we wear on the outside reflects who we are on the inside, which is the parent's call to target their hearts first.

What heart-developing character traits should a person have regarding modesty? Knowing what character traits you want to instill in a child's heart is of utmost importance because those characteristics will influence all of their external behavioral decisions. Think about what I'm suggesting in an inverted way: teach them how to behave or what they should wear without addressing their hearts. That approach is legalism, a horrible disservice to anyone. It's wiser to train their little hearts with Christlike character than mandating rote, choreographed clothing choices.

We wanted our children to learn essential character traits before focusing on behaviors. For example, respect, honor, gratitude, wisdom, discretion, and humility were a few essentials we wanted to instill into their little hearts. We saw these qualities as foundational early on, knowing we would come alongside them as they grew older, teaching them how to think and build biblical behaviors on top of those attributes, including modesty. Beauty is external, but respect, honor, gratitude, wisdom, discretion, and humility are rooted in the heart. If we did not begin in the right place, foundational speaking, our children could end up like pigs with gold rings stuck in their snouts.

Parents First

The all-important question is, where do you begin teaching your children these traits? The starting place is always in the parents' hearts. The teacher (parent) must internalize and practice the teaching they hope to export to their children. Otherwise, teaching a child about modesty would be hypocritical if we don't model and manifest our instruction. Children have ingrown baloney detectors. They can discern hypocritical parenting. We must not be full of baloney. We can fake them out for a season, but they will discern the disconnect between orthodoxy and orthopraxy as they grow older. May our example clearly represent the Christ we want them to emulate (Ephesians 5:1; 1 Corinthians 11:1). Our lives are the most potent examples of what will shape the future of our children. May I ask you a few questions about your modeling modesty to your children?

- Knowing that respect, honor, gratitude, wisdom, discretion, and humility are the feeders of future modesty, how would you rate yourself on these character traits? How would your spouse rate you?
- Are you modest? Jesus taught us that our fruit would reveal our hearts. What does your external presentation reveal about your heart?
- Are you tempted to conform to your culture? How much influence does the culture have over you? Do you look like them? Do you imitate your worldly counterparts?
- Who are your modesty mentors, e.g., movies, worldly friends, social media, godly people?
- Where did you learn about modesty? Was it through a religious system? Was it the Bible? Did someone come alongside you to help you understand biblical modesty?
- Have you overreacted to modesty teaching because of legalistic training? Are you guilty of pendulum swinging from legalism to liberality?
- What do these characteristics look like, practically speaking, in the home between a husband and wife? May I make a few appeals to illustrate this?

Appeal to Husbands

To do modesty well in the home means husbands and wives must be regularly and transparently talking about this culturally relevant issue. A husband and wife are more than two people; they are also one flesh—a covenantal union. Like Christ, the husband reflects his wife, and the wife reflects her husband. It would confuse a child if the parents revealed two different modesty messages. Regardless of where the split messages are, split marriages perpetuate confusion and insecurity in children. Kids are not mature enough to understand mixed marriage messages—when the parents are not in agreement about vital issues.

A couple becomes one voice in the child's life by developing a unified message consistent with their hearts. Single-mindedness in marriage means both partners must have authentic conversations that delve into the core of their respective selves. If those character traits are not there, the other spouse needs to understand why. What stands in place of them? Husband, your wife needs to know the real you. She needs to know your victories and struggles. She needs to understand the difference between the person you are and the one that everyone else knows. You should not give her all the gory details of your true self; be appropriate, but she must be a life partner who is permitted to enter your more personal struggles.

You can't expect to address your child's heart—teaching them what to be on the inside—when you are unwilling to reveal your heart to your wife. Your wife is your best ally—other than the Lord. It's incumbent on you to leverage this incredible asset. She is a gift to you. Use this means of grace from the Lord by letting her into your heart. Perhaps your marriage is not able to be this transparent at this time. Maybe you have not led her well. If that is true, I appeal to you to make one flesh unity one of your most important priorities.

Lead by example. Work at being as open and honest with your spouse as you want your child to be with you.

Appeal to Wives

For marriages to mature, both partners need to continuously press into each other to help the marriage reflect Christ and His church to their children. You want to make the gospel attractive to your children. Biblical attractiveness means the wife must know how her husband struggles with lust, sex, sexuality, and the temptation to take God's good gift of love and reverse it into a cursed-shaped, self-serving mindset. No man's view and practice of love are precisely like the mind of Christ. Imperfection makes him an ordinary fallen man in a fallen world.

Your husband is a product of Adam's race, though he is not a helpless victim. But he is a depraved man nonetheless. A good discipler will resist the temptation to become emotionally entangled in the problems of the person they are helping while bringing restorative care that transforms the person they are helping. As you come alongside your husband, make sure you address the real issues, which means you must think theologically more than emotionally. Rather than making his problems about your fears and insecurities, make them about God's ability to restore strugglers (Galatians 6:1-2).

Love your man. Help him rather than pulling away at the marriage bond. Give your children a marriage and message that values and manifests transparency, honesty, hope, and humility, which will determine their views on modesty. If your husband does not cooperate with this mission of modesty," I appeal to you to talk to your pastor or another spiritual authority (Matthew 17:15-17). Do all you can to close whatever gaps that exist between you and your husband. The goal here is not to bypass heart issues when teaching children what to look like on the outside.

Practical Modesty

LADIES: What are you trying to accomplish by what you are wearing? Whether you eat, drink, or dress, are you seeking to draw attention to God or yourself? (See 1 Corinthians 10:31.)

- Is your desire to make God's name great by your clothing choices?
- Do your clothes spread the fame of God to your family and community?
- Do you have a trusted, godly, and courageous female friend willing to speak to your clothing choices?
- Can you talk about the motivations of your heart pertaining to what you wear?

Your clothing selections begin in your heart, not on the rack. What you wear reveals who you are. Are you pursuing humility through your clothing choices? Recognize your tendencies toward self-deception, cultural pressures, and peer temptations. The subtleties of self-deception tempt all of us. The first step in understanding is acknowledging that it can happen to any of us. The humble person has nothing to hide, protect, or fear. Her goals are to learn, grow, change, and mature for the glory of God. Let these gentle provocations propel you to the safety of godly counsel (Proverbs 11:14).

GENTLEMEN: Let's be honest: lust tempts you and me. You are tempted toward ungodliness when it comes to the opposite sex. You may not yield to that temptation; I'm not saying you are, but it crouches at the door of all of our hearts. Sexual selfishness is part of our Adamic DNA. Can you talk about this universal problem that is every man's battle? To pretend it does not exist is to be naive, or even worse, it could be deceptive. Humble transparency about Adamic proclivities is the first step toward exporting modesty to the next generation.

Don't let your internal private struggles stay secret. Find a godly, wise, and trusted friend. Tell him the truth about the real you. Be released from the fear that you are the only one who struggles this way. You're not. Stop condoning men's meetings where every guy in the room thinks the same thing, but no one speaks up about their struggles. Shoot the lust elephant in the room. Tell the truth. If you and your wife are willing to pursue modesty through the door of humble and contrite hearts, you're well-positioned to export the message of modesty to your children.

Exporting the Message

As your children mature, you can incrementally increase their awareness of the dangers and pitfalls of modesty. Many parents may think, "We will never agree on this kind of modesty worldview. What divides us is too big. We can't talk about the simplest things; there is no way to expose our true functional identities." Non-redemptive Christian marriages are more commonplace than redemptive ones. Sin has done more damage in marriages than the sanctifying gospel has restored. If this is your situation, you should not be hopeless. If you are hopeless, I want you to think about those two words: Hopeless Christian. Does that sound right to you?

Hopeless and Christian do not belong in the same contiguous breath. If you feel hopeless, the first thing you need to do is repent. Your problems are not greater than God's ability to repair them. Begin the hard work of transforming your thoughts back to the redemptive power of the gospel. The Son of God died on a cross. He came out of the grave three days later. Let those gospel-saturated words course through your mind. Regardless of what your spouse does, you can have renewed thinking (Ephesians

4:23). Don't be like Mary at the tomb, languishing in despair (John 20:11).

Christ did rise just like He said He would (Matthew 28:6), and you know the message of hope. Preach it to yourself right now. You can do better than hopelessness. Perhaps your spouse will not help you export modesty to your children. If that is so, think about this: all you need is God. The message of grace alone applies here, too. If your child comes to a place of embracing modesty for the glory of God, it will be because of His grace, not because of your beautiful marriage or exceptional parenting practices (Ephesians 2:8-9). There are two ditches here:

- Not cooperating with God in exporting modesty to your children (Philippians 2:12-13).
- Your failures are not more significant than God's power to transform a child's heart.

The first problem is presuming on the grace of God (Psalm 19:13), while the second one is self-righteous legalism. Let sound theology govern your heart. You do the best you can while always resting in the sweet assurance that God will care for you. Believe in and practice the active goodness of God in your life; may He be your animating center.

Call to Action

1. Why is it essential to begin with your heart when teaching your children modesty?
2. What character traits would you add to my list?
3. Why is it vital for the husband and wife to be honest, transparent, and vulnerable about themselves?
4. What is the pitfall of being one thing on the inside while mandating Christian deportment on the outside?
5. What is the danger of a mixed marriage message in which the husband lives and teaches one way and the wife lives another way? How are your children experiencing your unified marriage modesty message?
6. How does legalism affect your thoughts about modesty?
7. If you have messed up as parents, which is more significant in your thinking—God's grace or your mistakes? Why did you answer that way?

10

Modesty Wars

Too often, discussions about modesty digress into contentious sparring matches between Christians with differing perspectives on secondary issues. Usually, it's the legalist and the liberal thinking believer, a sad commentary about our Christian maturity in light of the horrendous things that are happening all around us. We can be like kids arguing over the bigger piece of candy when these privileged sugar fixes are less common in many parts of the world where having anything to eat is a daily struggle. In a culture like ours, where we've been spoiled for so long, the tendency to devolve into less weighty matters speaks to how easily our hearts curve into themselves.

For God's Fame

So, whether you eat or drink, or whatever you do, do all to the glory of God.

(1 Corinthians 10:31)

Wearing clothes is an everyday experience, and how we think about the apparel we wear is a biblically and culturally relevant issue, especially in light of our call to spread the fame of God to a fallen world. To glorify God means to spread His fame throughout the world by making His name fabulously great in our sphere of influence. Paul might say, "Whether we eat, drink, or wear clothes,

God calls us to do all of those things for God's glory." We should have a magnification of the Lord focus, which is an all-encompassing command that even brings our clothing choices under the rubric of spreading God's fame. David talked about it this way: "Oh, magnify the Lord with me, and let us exalt his name together" (Psalm 34:3)!

We are like a modern-day John the Baptist, the guy who stood in the wilderness pointing people to Christ (John 3:28, 30). His job description is ours, too. The life we live is an ongoing process of learning how to decrease while intentionally increasing the person and work of Christ so others can hear and respond to the message of the gospel. When thinking about the clothes we wear, the most appropriate place to begin is in our hearts, specifically with our motivations. Perhaps a few questions may assist us in aligning our thoughts about clothing and motive. How would you answer these?

- Are you aware of how your motives influence what you wear?
- You could ask the question in reverse: How do your clothing choices reflect your motives?
- What do your clothes say about you as a person?
- What do your clothes say about your relationship with God?
- Do you crave affection, love, or acceptance and use your clothes as a means to gain those things?

Christians are missionaries. If you are a Christian, you are an alien living on foreign soil for the purpose of convincing earthlings to worship your King. The practical way we live our life matters as much as the message we communicate. Listen to Peter.

Beloved, I urge you as sojourners and exiles to abstain from the passions of the flesh, which wage

war against your soul. Keep your conduct among the
Gentiles honorable, so that when they speak against
you as evildoers, they may see your good deeds and
glorify God on the day of visitation.

(1 Peter 2:11-12)

The Modesty Wars

Christians are influencing their culture for Christ, or their
culture is affecting them for Satan. Our clothing choices are
one practical way we can discern if we are influencing them
or if they are influencing us. Our clothes are messages that
either work in tandem with the message of the gospel or
work in conjunction with the ways of the world. Clothes are
not neutral garments hanging on the Christian missionary.
Regrettably, this tension about our clothes creates modesty
wars within the Christian community. There are several
factions in this war. For this chapter, I have separated the
camps into two general groups—the conservatives (legalists)
and the non-conservatives (liberals). My conservative
friends clearly see the dangers of dressing sensually. They
are not blind, and I do not disagree with them. Calling them
legalistic while entirely dismissing their perspectives is
myopic and immature.

My legalistic friends are like the rest of us in that
they have problems, too, but when it comes to clothing
choices, they are typically more clear-headed than the
non-conservative Christian community. The conservative
Christian community knows that sex sells, and they are
soberly aware of how so many of their brothers and sisters
are promoting the sensual agenda of our culture. As a
counselor, I've had the opportunity to see their complaint
in a clearer way than most people. Sensual thinking and
attire are nearly always associated with adultery, porn, and
many other marital problems, including divorce. What our
conservative friends are observing in our culture is a serious

matter that is unarguable. Adultery, porn, and divorce are not isolated behavioral events that have no relation to a person's heart motivations or lifestyle choices.

Nobody falls into adultery. No one makes an out-of-the-blue decision to live a lifestyle of porn. There is always a long trail that leads to these patterns, and the trailhead is always in the sensual person's heart. With every sensual family problem I have dealt with, there were sensual patterns of the heart that were in place long before anyone knew about the person's sinful lifestyle. My conservative friends are correct in their observations. If they do err, it is an overreactive response to their observations—a sheltering in place behind thick-walled barricades—that dissociates themselves from the culture they should penetrate. You may not agree with how our conservative friends dress themselves, but it would be short-sighted to say what they are observing in the culture and among other Christians is wrong.

Go Get Jesus

Because some of our conservative, legalistic friends over-correct their clothing choices, they end up drawing attention away from sensuality while drawing attention to their counter-cultural attire. Though their intentions may be good, their clothing ends up distracting the culture from the gospel message. It is possible to draw attention to yourself by dressing in such a way that you become a hindrance to the gospel. Jesus did not dress weirdly out of step with His culture. He was a relevant guy who knew how to relate to His culture. Jesus did not dress counter-culturally, and He did not dress immodestly. Jesus was not flashy or showy, and He did not dress in such a conservative fashion that His clothes were more of a talking point than His gospel.

When someone spent time with Jesus, they said, "No

one ever spoke like this man," rather than, "No one ever dressed like this man." (See John 7:46.) There was nothing about Christ's appearance that distracted His audience from His message. He fit into His culture. He was not in the conservative or the liberal camp. He was outside both camps (Hebrews 13:13), walking in a way that drew attention to His message. There were times when people could not find Christ in a crowd because He looked like the crowd (Matthew 26:48). I want to be more like Christ, where people are more aware of my character and message than my clothing choices.

> Do not let your adorning be external—the braiding of hair and the putting on of gold jewelry, or the clothing you wear—but let your adorning be the hidden person of the heart with the imperishable beauty of a gentle and quiet spirit, which in God's sight is very precious.
>
> (1 Peter 3:3-4)

My Legalistic Friends

Sadly, my conservative and liberal Christian friends have their respective ditches where they hunker down while tossing grenades at the other side. My conservative friends, who have an unbiblical view of worldliness, dress as opposite as possible from their culture. My anti-conservative friends, who have an unbiblical view of modesty, dress as opposite as possible from their conservative friends. For example, when you wear culottes to the beach or dresses on a ski slope, you are not making God's name great. That is analogous to the Corinthians speaking in tongues in a church meeting without an interpreter. It wasn't very clear to the non-Christian community of Paul's day what those weird people were doing other than impeding the message of Christ.

If, therefore, the whole church comes together and all speak in tongues, and outsiders or unbelievers enter, will they not say that you are out of your minds?
(1 Corinthians 14:23)

Out-of-date or counter-culture clothing choices do not, by and large, point unregenerate people to Christ. The cross of Christ is foolish enough (1 Corinthians 1:18). We don't need to place hurdles in front of the cross that confuse, distract, or hinder our unregenerate friends from getting to the cross. Non-relevant attire becomes a cultural anomaly that may garner a few looks, but the quizzical onlooker typically dismisses the conservative person or marginalizes them through mocking or devaluation. Either way, it's the clothes that gain the attention more than the magnification of Christ.

Mocking conservative clothing choices is what happened to me before I became a Christian. I thought being a Christian meant I had to ride a bicycle and wear black slacks and shoes, with a white shirt and black tie. I assumed I had to have a badge on my white shirt that said, "Elder Rick." I did not know Mormons weren't Christians, but what I did know was that I did not want to be like them, not for theological reasons, but because of their weird clothing choices. Their anti-culture dress standards made no sense to me. Their message got lost in their apparel. In hindsight, it was not a bad thing that their clothing choices turned me away from their message.

My Hyper-grace Friends

But take care that this right of yours does not somehow become a stumbling block to the weak.
(1 Corinthians 8:9)

Guard your heart so that your freedom in Christ is not a stumbling block to your weaker brothers and sisters in

Christ who sincerely believe they are right on this issue of modesty. (See 1 Corinthians 8.) Too many of my non-conservative friends have overreacted to the legalism. Many of them were part of the legalistic culture before seeing the light. Their overreaction is what I call the grace mistake. They have become overly focused on the legalism they came out of, which tempts some of them to react by going too far into a non- (or sub-) Christian liberality. They misunderstand biblical freedom as they react to what they disdain. By distancing themselves from their conservative past, they unwittingly yoke themselves to their culture.

If you're in the liberal trap, I appeal to you to reconsider how you think about your legalistic friends. Love them, and while you're doing so, ensure you are not distracting your unregenerate friends from the point and purpose of the gospel. They need to know Christ more than your coolness. Christianity is not supposed to be hip. The message of the cross is as anti-cultural as it can be. Christianity is a death march. It's a call to die to yourself. You should have a counter-cultural heart condition, which should drive all your choices. Paul and Peter were clear on how our calling to Christ should be counter-intuitive to cultural norms. As you live out coolness for the cause of Christ, make sure you model something far superior to your cultural relevance and hipness. Our world needs to see the hope we have in Christ.

> For it has been granted to you that for the sake of Christ you should not only believe in him but also suffer for his sake.
>
> (Philippians 1:29)

> For to this, you have been called, because Christ also suffered for you, leaving you an example, so that you might follow in his steps.
>
> (1 Peter 2:21)

Final Appeal

Joseph was the sexiest slave in Egypt. He had no church, no Bible, no friends, no church clothes, and no help. But God was with him, and it was obvious to all (Genesis 39:2). In one of the most isolated times of his life, he did not look Christian, but everyone knew God was with him. How about you? How does your life communicate that God is with you? Do your clothes get in the way of the message of Christ? The Savior was a root out of the dry ground, and there was no beauty that we should desire Him (Isaiah 53). Rather than getting a makeover, He stayed the course and went to His death, and even today, He is turning the world upside down.

> Therefore I tell you, do not be anxious about your life, what you will eat or what you will drink, nor about your body, what you will put on. Is not life more than food, and the body more than clothing?
> (Matthew 6:25)

Is the main thing—the gospel—the main thing in your life? Spreading God's fame is more important than what we wrap around our bodies. Do not err by your legalism or your liberality. Guard your heart, love your God, serve your neighbor, and send an unobstructed message to your world. I encourage you to dress in such a way that does not capture the gaze of any person. It matters not if you're male or female. Our Christian duty is to point people to Christ. We are signposts in the wilderness. If your conservative clothing distracts from the message of Christ, consider changing your clothing style. If your culturally relevant clothing distracts from the message of Christ, consider changing your clothing style.

Call to Action

1. Have you over-corrected from one style to another? If so, how so, and what would be the right way for you to present the glory of Christ to your culture?

2. Do you know how to blend into your culture while communicating a counter-cultural message? Please explain.

3. When people see you, do they know you are different—not by what you wear, but because God is with you? You have a quality that draws people to Jesus.

4. The best-dressed person looks like the fruit of the Spirit. Will you read Galatians 5:22-23 and speak with a friend about how you emulate each of those nine elements of the Spirit's fruit in your life?

11

What My Wife Wears

As you might imagine, when writing a book on sex, temptation, and modesty and talking to a few friends about the project elicits lively conversation, including what a person wears at the beach or around their pools. And why not? The Bible provides all we need for life and godliness, including beachwear. Though what you wear to the beach is a tertiary matter, our clothing choices should never be divorced from community input. Our physical bodies are part of a greater body of Christ that requires a corporate responsibility of putting the beauty of Christ on display in a fallen culture, making the beach question a relevant one. No Christian should say, "It's none of your business." Christians must not be that rude or aloof. We care for each other, which is why I want to share a question put to me about our beach clothes.

Practical Modesty

Rick, I have enjoyed your book on modesty. It has been helpful and convicting. You talked a lot about the heart and theory, but may I ask a more practical question? What is your stand regarding swimsuits? I know bikinis are immodest (underwear covers more than that). As a

Christian, I've struggled with this issue for my kids, as well as for myself, for a long time. We've required one-piece suits with dark T-shirts, but this is not enough in my view. I strive for our family to be modest without being irrelevant to our society. The balance between fitting in and not compromising biblical expectations is a challenge. I'd love to hear another opinion from a like-minded believer.

Practical modesty is a tough question for me to answer because it's a secondary matter that releases every believer to be free in Christ to choose what they want to wear to the beach. There are also cultural considerations, making Americans different from Europeans, and so forth. The tension for me is that some people could interpret my way as *the* way, which is not my heart. When I write, I'm sensitive to my audience, and I'm aware that I'm not speaking of an American-exclusive audience. Also, the more I travel, the more I realize that secondary issues vary so much that we should be careful about making blanket statements where the Bible is not explicit. With topics like these, I attempt to communicate the importance of the articles *the* and *a* carefully. There is *a way* of doing things, and there is *the way* of doing things.

The "What should I wear to the beach?" question falls under *a way* of decision-making, not *the way*. Understanding an "article question" is an enormous and necessary distinction we must make. We cannot insist that our expectations and preferences are for every Christian. I have an opinion on beach clothes, and so do you, but nobody should upload my opinion as the final word. My friend's question about our beach attire is humble, though. Even though there is purposeful freedom across the Christian spectrum to pick and choose what we wear, we should never dismiss the importance of community collaboration on secondary matters. Our humility should always lead the way, motivating us to seek wisdom from other believers.

Purposeful Freedom

You are free to do what you believe is the right thing for you and your family. Of course, I'm not the first person you should ask, which is why I assume you have already discussed this with your spouse—your co-collaborator in life. My wife is the first person that I would ask because we are one flesh, which makes her opinion essential in our family discussions. I would also recommend you talk to your children about this—assuming they are old enough and mature enough to weigh in on these "gray area" conversations. I imagine you have. Those who are most affected by your decision should be part of your decision. Collaboration does not mean you strictly follow your children's perspectives, but it is a way to honor and respect them by inviting them into this discussion.

Several years ago, Lucia and I began the complex and challenging decision-making process of attending another church. As we were nearing the end of the process, we let our children know where we were with our decision-making and then asked their thoughts about a church change. Our youngest daughter asked, "Why are you asking us since you're going to do what you want to do anyway?" I suspect her question could sound rude or disrespectful, but it was not. She was humbly asking out of curiosity. She was confused as to why we were talking to them about changing churches because she ultimately knew we would do what we thought was best for our family. Her query presented an excellent opportunity to walk her through parent/child dynamics and collaboration. I told her that our conversation about a church change is similar to how we relate to the Lord.

Ultimately, the Lord is going to do what He wants to do with our lives, but that does not mean He's a disinterested Deity. He desires to relate to us. He wants to hear from us. He wants interactive, loving, communicative relationships with His children, and that is what I want with our children. Yes, I will lead our family, but not as a distant, dismissive, or disinterested dad. I want our children's participation, even though I'm soberly aware God mandates me to lead them. She understood this perspective and was gracious in our discussions. Your children will understand, too, and they will respect you for encouraging them to participate in family discussions, especially on culturally relevant topics like this one.

> You shall love the Lord your God with all your heart and with all your soul and with all your mind. This is the great and first commandment. And a second is like it: You shall love your neighbor as yourself.
> (Matthew 22:37-39)

What Our Children Wear

As our kids were heading into their teen years, we had already had many discussions about clothing and their choices. We did not wait until they were teenagers before establishing a worldview and expectations. Though our children are far from perfect, we have been intentional in teaching them an across-the-board worldview about loving God and others throughout their lives. It's important to begin teaching your children a "love God and others" worldview before they can walk and talk. It's similar to the sex talk. You begin teaching a sex worldview when they are toddlers by how you relate to your spouse. Similarly, if your first discussions about beach clothing are when your children are teenagers, it's too late. They have cemented worldviews and presuppositions by that time.

In the early years, a parent's worldview-shaping teaching is more conceptual than practical. The initial parenting goal is to build a theoretical basis for future practical matters. Parents walk their kids through the practical aspects as they grow older. Some of those foundational and conceptual ideas are respect, honor, discretion, and humility. Of course, the parent must be modeling these characteristics in their marriages. How we interact with our spouses will help or hinder who we connect respect, discretion, and other fruit of the Spirit ideas in the minds of our children. These early concepts are important because you want to shape their minds regarding the two best commandments: love God and love others more than loving themselves.

If you lay a foundation of respect, honor, discretion, and humility, they will be ready when teen temptations come knocking. Before the teen years, our children only knew about the concept of modesty. Because fear of man was not that big of a problem, the temptations of cultural norms and expectations did not resonate with them. The preteen years were more about jumping in the ocean and digging in the sand, while the teen years were more about looking good at the beach. The early training regarding these character traits paid off when they were older. While our children wanted to blend with their culture by being relevant, they were not interested in looking sexy. Thus, our daughters wore one-piece swimsuits, and most of the time, they wore shorts to cover their bottoms.

Submission & Protection

SPIRITUAL SUBMISSION: Lucia has excelled in teaching our daughters to ask my opinion about their clothing preferences. She also models this personally; she wants my opinion and input about her clothes. She has trained our daughters to seek my advice, which has served our girls well, and we hope that humility will carry over into their marriages. Spiritual submission and biblical leadership are essential for any marriage or family to function well.

Physical protection: There are the physical dangers of being in the sun. Honestly, I don't want skin cancer, so I don't go to the beach without a T-shirt-type swim top. Our entire family has done this for years. I'm not sexually tempting to anyone, and I couldn't care less about that, but I do care a lot about skin cancer. We all have nice, fitting, and cool-looking swimwear that protects our bodies from the damage of the sun.

> Do nothing from selfish ambition or conceit, but in humility count others more significant than yourselves. Let each of you look not only to his own interests but also to the interests of others.
>
> (Philippians 2:3-4)

What My Wife Wears

Lucia humbly models an exceptional love for God and others. As we have talked about modesty for this book, our conversations reignited things that are vital to each of us. She told me the other day how she appreciates my input because she does not know how to think like a man. Before our children's teen years, I did not go in-depth with them about sex, sensuality, and sex-related issues. After they became young adults, we did launch into more detailed discussions. With Lucia, it has been different; I have talked at length with her for multiple decades about sex, sexuality, and temptation. Lucia is my greatest ally and my most effective disciple-maker—as she cares for me, which is why she needs to know about men and sexual temptation.

More importantly, she needs to know about me and my weaknesses, temptations, and failures. Her awareness not only helps her to care for me, but it also helps us as parents to effectively lead and shape our children to live well in God's world after they mature into independent adults. Thus, what Lucia wears to the beach begins in her heart, and the two main things that control her heart are spiritual and physical carefulness. To put it plainly, she does not want to dress sexually tempting for others, and she does not want to die of skin cancer. Lucia dresses for the beach like the rest of our family. Her humility motivates her to model the expectations she has for her children and her husband.

For us, the beach is about pleasure for our family, function in and out of the water, and modeling a relevant Jesus to those around us. While we want to have a good time and we want to be able to swim with relative ease, we do hope that what we wear does not draw unnecessary attention to ourselves. Drawing attention to ourselves by over-modesty or by giving sneak peeks of our sexuality are not biblical goals. We have one modesty goal, which is to put the beauty of Christ on display. Dressing in a way that the culture interprets as weird does not do that. Dressing in a way that captures the lusty looks of others does not do that. The modesty sweet spot is not to bring positive or negative attention to ourselves through what we wear but to draw engagement through how we interact with our family and the culture around us.

Call to Action

Modesty is more than a "what we wear" issue; it's a worldview that plummets the depth of our hearts while extending across the spectrum of all the people within our sphere of influence. How you think about God and others matters most. The foundational ideas of honor, respect, discretion, kindness, love, and humility will determine where you land on the modesty question. You must begin with those character traits before you start addressing your clothing choices. Everything Jesus did poured out of His humility, discretion, love, kindness, and other fruit of the Spirit categories. (See 1 Corinthians 13:4-7 and Galatians 5:22-23.)

1. When you think about your beach clothes, do you begin with your heart or your clothes? Please explain.
2. Are the characteristics of your heart humility, love, respect, and discretion? I'm not asking if you have perfected these things, but would you say the presence of these traits characterizes you? One of the ways you can answer this question is by submitting your clothing choices to a trusted, courageous, and loving spiritual friend. Will you do that?
3. After reading this book, is there anything you need to change regarding your heart or your clothes? If so, what is your specific plan for change? Who will you talk to, asking them to hold you accountable to persevere through what changes you need to make?

About the Author

 Rick Thomas launched the Life Over Coffee global training network in 2008 to bring hope and help for you and others by creating resources that spark conversations for transformation. His primary responsibilities are resource creation and leadership development, which he does through speaking, writing, podcasting, and educating. In 1990 he earned a BA in Theology and, in 1991, a BS in Education. In 1993, he received his ordination into Christian ministry, and in 2000, he graduated with an MA in Counseling from The Master's University. In 2006, he was recognized as a Fellow of the Association of Certified Biblical Counselors (ACBC).

Other Books Available from
Life Over Coffee

Boasting in Weakness
Centering Your Marriage on Christ
Communication
Complete Marriage
Don't Apologize
Exchange the Truth for a Lie
Help My Marriage Has Grown Cold
Identity Crisis
Local Church
Loving Me
Mad
Marriage Devotion We Are One
Politics and Culture
Parenting Devotion from Zero to Adulthood
Sex, Temptation, and Modesty
Storm Hurler
The Cyber Effect
The Talk
Wives Leading
You Decide

www.ingramcontent.com/pod-product-compliance
Lightning Source LLC
Chambersburg PA
CBHW071524120626
46550CB00006B/2354